DATE DUE

JY 3 0 '98 MR 2 6 '0?		
OC 2 5 '98 AO 1 3 '98		
NO 1 8 '98		
MY 2 0 '99		
JE 1 0 '80		
DE 1 3 00		
OE 2 0		
MY 1 8 '01		
DE 19 01		
DE 1 6 '02		
JE 1 1 03		
OC 3 1 '03		

Bobbi Kendig, MSW, LCSW
with Clara Lowry, MSW, ACSW, LCSW

Cedar House
A Model Child Abuse Treatment Program

*Pre-publication
REVIEWS,
COMMENTARIES,
EVALUATIONS . . .*

"**T**his book is like nothing else in the literature on child abuse. More than a model or a history, *Cedar House* is a vision, an insider's guide to a higher consciousness and greater confidence in caring. Bobbi Kendig's candid, engaging style eases the reader into the heart and soul of dysfunctional families, buoyed always with a respect and optimism that promises constructive solutions. Eager students and jaded veterans in all of the helping professions will be inspired and enlightened by this wonderful book."

Roland C. Summit, MD
Psychiatrist and Clinical Associate Professor Emeritus, Harbor/UCLA Medical Center, Torrance, CA

"**T**he authors have provided a thoughtful description of building and maintaining a neighborhood model of human engagement, with all its strengths and blemishes. Cedar House is truly a model child abuse treatment program. The book provides theory, techniques, guidelines, problems, solutions, and case studies, but most of all a healthy underlying respect for human beings and their struggle to survive.

This book is a must for students and advanced professionals involved in the field of child abuse and for those who care about starting where the client is.

Cedar House provided an anchor for families in the midst of a tidal wave. The staff and volunteers went hand in hand with families into their homes, to court, to the doctor, to wherever was needed.

This book is not about one-hour-a-week, private outpatient psychotherapy, but contains the essence, the bones, the meat, and the muscle of what is needed in working with families of abuse.

I had the privilege of substituting for Bobbi Kendig one summer at Cedar House and it changed my professional life permanently."

Suzanne Long, MSW
Private Counselor,
Newport Beach, CA

"**C**edar House is a 'how to' book for conducting a child-abuse program. If such a subject can be dealt with in a personal and even charming manner, Bobbi Kendig has done it. The difficulties of starting, building, and maintaining the program are carefully detailed but the focus is on the parents battling urges to vent their rage on their children. Staff members do not take an 'I know best' attitude but act naturally, as when two therapists disagreed, then resolved an argument in front of clients, who expected physical violence. Among the many poignant stories is that of Sandy: depressed and reclusive, she would not have come but for the staff driving her to the first meeting; she remained silent until she ended up appointing herself social hostess for the final party."

Arthur Kraft, PhD
Retired Senior Psychologist,
Long Beach Unified Schools,
Long Beach, CA

"**B**obbi and Clara are pioneers in the field of child abuse. Cedar House was built with their love and concern. They were open, creative, and asked questions. They discovered what worked and used it. I remember the open door, a cozy living room atmosphere, the coffee pot always on and often the smell of cookies baking in the oven. This was an experience of a home that many parents had missed and did not know how to provide for their children. People shared their laughter and gifts but most importantly the deepest secrets, shame, rage, and tears of childhood abuse. Bobbi and Clara were undaunted and unafraid. They shared the very essence of excellent clinical social work . . . a deep respect for the clients and their innate ability to choose to grow. Cedar House offered to the community of Long Beach the very best of professional expertise and personal commitment."

Elizabeth Maris Kelley, LCSW
Clinical Social Worker,
St. Joseph Medical Center,
Reading, PA

"**W**hen Bobbi Kendig and Clara Lowry founded Cedar House, I was the Director of the Region IX Center on Child Abuse and Neglect. One of the objectives of the Center was to locate model child abuse preventive treatment programs. At that time, Cedar House was the only program exclusively dedicated to treating abused and/or neglected children and their families. I took the model program concepts and methods developed at Cedar House and disseminated them throughout Federal Region IX and the entire country.

I could transport the concepts, but I could not transport the positive, unyielding faith in all humans that Bobbi and Clara displayed. They truly were able to realize the saying that we are our brother's keepers. Their spirit permeates this volume and that spirit of caring is what always makes the difference for people in painful situations."

Hershel K. Swinger, PhD
Clinical Director,
Children's Institute International,
Los Angeles, CA

The Haworth Maltreatment and Trauma Press
An Imprint of The Haworth Press, Inc.
New York • London

Cedar House
A Model Child Abuse Treatment Program

THE HAWORTH MALTREATMENT AND TRAUMA PRESS
Robert A. Geffner, PhD
Senior Editor

New, Recent, and Forthcoming Titles:

Sexual, Physical, and Emotional Abuse in Out-of-Home Care: Prevention Skills for At-Risk Children by Toni Cavanagh Johnson and Associates

Cedar House: A Model Child Abuse Treatment Program by Bobbi Kendig with Clara Lowry

Bridging Worlds: Understanding and Facilitating Adolescent Recovery from the Trauma of Abuse by Joycee Kennedy and Carol McCarthy

The Learning About Myself (LAMS) Program for At-Risk Parents: Learning from the Past—Changing the Future by Verna Rickard

The Learning About Myself (LAMS) Handbook for Group Participants by Verna Rickard

Cedar House
A Model Child Abuse Treatment Program

Bobbi Kendig, MSW, LCSW
with Clara Lowry, MSW, ACSW, LCSW

The Haworth Maltreatment and Trauma Press
An Imprint of The Haworth Press, Inc.
New York • London

Published by

The Haworth Maltreatment and Trauma Press, an imprint of The Haworth Press, Inc., 10 Alice Street, Binghamton, NY 13904-1580

Cover design by Marylouise E. Doyle.

Library of Congress Cataloging-in-Publication Data

Kendig, Bobbi.
    Cedar House : a model child abuse treatment program / Bobbi Kendig : with Clara Lowry.
        p.   cm.
    Includes bibliographical references and index.
    ISBN 0-7890-0146-2 (alk. paper).
    1. Cedar House (Long Beach, Calif.). 2. Abused children—Services for—California—Long Beach. 3. Abusive parents—Services for—California—Long Beach. 4. Child abuse—California—Long Beach—Prevention. 5. Child abuse—California—Long Beach—Treatment. 6. Family social work—California—Long Beach—Case studies. I. Lowry, Clara. II. Title.
HV6626.53.C2K46 1998
362.76'85'0979493—dc21   97-37004
                                                                                            CIP

To the families who taught us how to treat them

ABOUT THE AUTHORS

Bobbi Kendig, MSW, LCSW, and **Clara Lowry, MSW, ACSW, LCSW,** serve as a team in private therapy practice, Lowry with parents and Kendig with the children, in Long Beach, California. They have been working together in counseling efforts for over twenty years. In 1974, they co-founded Cedar House, a program in Long Beach, California, for the treatment and prevention of child abuse and neglect. After Cedar House was chosen, in 1979, to be the model for Los Angeles County's network of Neighborhood Family Centers, Kendig and Lowry became consultants to those centers and to a private fundraising arm of Los Angeles County's Interagency Council on Child Abuse and Neglect, ICAN Associates. In 1984, they co-founded Sarah Center, a treatment program for young sexually abused children and their families, in Long Beach. From 1991 to 1993, they served as consultants to Friends Outside, a program serving prisoners, parolees, and their families. And, under the auspices of Friends Outside, they established a therapeutic program for families of prisoners and parolees, providing group and individual therapy for adults and children.

CONTENTS

Foreword

In 1974 an unlikely spirit was moving in Los Angeles County. It was as prescient as it was unprecedented: it signaled the fledgling promise of a new era in child abuse awareness and child protection. This upstart *Zeitgeist* was materializing in every aspect of community structure, from self-help gatherings to social services, health and mental health agencies, and law enforcement—even to the chambered aeries of county government.

Both the Los Angeles Police Department and the County Sheriff's Department had developed special child abuse intervention teams, with officers Jackie Howell and Carol Walker Painter, respectively, sparkplugging those agendas. Deputy District Attorney Jean Matusinka had established an unofficial domestic violence task force among prosecutors. These three visionaries established a series of monthly brown bag lunch meetings with previously unfamiliar downtown colleagues who worked in education, child protective services, and children's health services. Such unprecedented teamwork proved to be both innovative and indispensable. The meetings evolved into an enduring public-private institution: The Interagency Council on Child Abuse and Neglect (ICAN).

In the South Bay area another unlikely partnership had engendered a new concept in child protection: professional/parental self-help. A desperately demanding mother later known as "Jolly K" rose to the challenge of her frustrated state social services counselor, Leonard Lieber. If available agencies cannot save the life of your daughter from your homicidal frenzies, he reasoned, there must be other abusive parents who can learn to help one another. Together, counselor and client, they founded Parents Anonymous.

As Jolly K had discovered, the help of professionals in the 1960s and early 1970s was often worse than no help at all in confronting the unfamiliar specter of child abuse. Increasing sophistication and teamwork in identifying and removing children-at-risk tended to demonize abusive parents as aliens from traditional treatment resources. Family guidance clinics of the time had no facility for parents too conflicted and too embattled to present themselves for guilt-provoking clinical appraisal.

The revolution waiting to happen in 1974 was actually an evolution of consciousness born some ten years before. Child abuse itself had been officially "discovered" only in 1961 with the publication of *The Battered Child Syndrome*. The traumatic fallout of that end of innocence filtered into medical, nursing, and social work curricula at the same time that the social revolution of the 1960s challenged traditional concepts of professional roles and responsibilities.

Students in the University of Southern California School of Social Work were soaking up an imperative for outreach and the idealization of change. I came to know at least three of those fresh faces, all masters graduates of the Class of 1966, as community professionals who stood out in a class by themselves through their unique vision, initiative, and compassion. One of these was a champion for interagency teamwork and home visitation with the impossible-to-reach families we encountered through the South Bay Professional Case Conference. That was Leonard Lieber, who went on to cofound Parents Anonymous. The two other classmates were Bobbi Kendig and Clara Lowry, who would abandon the security of office employment in 1974 to found Cedar House.

These two masters of social work could not master the problems of child abuse as office-based counselors, either in the public Bureau of Public Assistance or in a private adolescent residential facility called Trailback Lodge. They wondered if lives could be saved and families redeemed through community outreach within a more client-empathic, more accessible resource.

An unfulfilled plan for a Trailback shelter for runaway youth provided another unlikely alliance and the venue for a new concept in community caring: the masters of social work met a mistress of the house. Marilyn Johnson had been recruited as house mother for the runaway shelter. With no professional training or counseling experience, she offered the kind of calm, warm, intuitive, common sense that could offer bonding and support to families in trouble. Just as important, as it turned out, were her kitchen skills. Marilyn's knack for filling a house with olfactory icons like fresh-brewed coffee and fresh-from-the-oven cinnamon rolls afforded a subliminal promise of the kind of nurturant environment most clients could barely imagine.

So it was with Cedar House: a professional/parent partnership that offered an attractive, therapeutic, child-protective haven for parents and children desperately in need of caring.

The spirit of 1974 has endured in the many partnerships forged in that galvanic era. Jolly K became a member of the ICAN Policy Council, sitting side-by-side and eye-to-eye with chiefs of police and agency directors. Clara and Bobbi helped reinvigorate the Long Beach Child Trauma Council, which became the template for child abuse councils throughout California. Cedar House became the model for ICAN Neighborhood Family Stress Centers, a standard of excellence and effectiveness that has outlived Cedar House itself.

But the real essence of Cedar House cannot be captured fairly in protocols and requests for grant proposals. The homelike atmosphere suffused with Marilyn's comforts, the dining room table group intakes, the home visits and crisis outreach, the down-to-earth humility and common sense coupled with a no-nonsense professional scrutiny—these are the spirituous vapors that are too easily evaporated in the natural preference for familiar and more comfortable professional roles and institutional boundaries.

It is the recapturing of that evanescent spirit that makes this book at once essential and unique. There is a vast new literature on the etiology and treatment of child abuse, much of it research-based and experience-proven. Yet most current therapies presume an office base designed first for the comfort and convenience of the therapists. Abusive crises happen elsewhere, outside of offices and beyond the usual hours. And the most recently abusive parents will be the last to show up for the next scheduled appointment. This is not a book for nine-to-five hirelings. It is not a guide for designing and supervising generic family services. It is not a product of the latest research (although it anticipates and underscores the most modern enlightenment). It is up-to-date for the very fact that its model may appear to be out-of-date.

Cedar House, the book, offers a renaissance of lost arts. Bobbi Kendig and Clara Lowry invite your participation in a quiet revolution of consciousness. If child abuse is a human problem, if parenting is a home-based, intergenerational tradition that needs emergency intervention when children are neglected or endangered, if agency professionals are at risk of being overqualified and inaccessible to the clients who are most in need, then I believe there is no better formula for rewarding, successful interaction than the Cedar House neighborhood model of human engagement.

Roland C. Summit, MD

Acknowledgments

Clara and I give heartfelt thanks to: Roland Summit, who provided the encouragement that got us started, who sustained us through the long process of putting the book together, and who added his own memories of our early days together; to Michael Durfee and Deanne Tilton Durfee of the Los Angeles Council on Child Abuse and Neglect, for their support through the years and for their sharing of memories of Cedar House; to Christina Crawford and to Morris Paulson of UCLA Neuropsychiatric Institute, each of whom urged us long ago to write about Cedar House and planted the seeds that finally bore fruit; to pediatrician Mark Goodman, who timed it right when he urged us to write; to Bond Johnson and Elizabeth Kraft, who gave us permission to start Cedar House; to Arthur Kraft, who provided valuable comments both on the content and on the technical aspects of the writing; to my son and daughter, David Kendig and Lisa Black, for their much-needed help on the use of the computer; and to the people—staff members, clients and volunteers, visitors and supporters, political figures and celebrities, and those too numerous to name, rich and poor, of all colors, types, and social classes—who entered our door and left their imprint on Cedar House.

I also thank my husband, Ed, and all three of our offspring, David, Susan, and Lisa, for their patience and loving support during the Cedar House years and ever since. They have been instrumental in helping me to maintain perspective.

Introduction

Clara Lowry, Marilyn Johnson, and I had no idea what we were getting into when we started Cedar House, a program for treating abused children and their families. That was a good thing, for if we had known, I doubt that we would have had the nerve.

In May 1974 Clara and I, both social workers, unlicensed at the time, had a conversation that was to be the beginning of this breathtaking journey. Clara had been working with a family in which one of two children had been killed by the mother. The mother was subsequently sentenced to prison and her surviving child sent to a foster home. Clara questioned whether the tragedy could have been averted had there been more emotional support for the mother.

Meanwhile, I was conducting a class in "filial therapy," teaching mothers to do play therapy with their own children. Having taken such a class under the tutelage of Dr. Arthur Kraft, a psychologist with the Long Beach Unified School District, I had found it to be a powerful tool for parents to get in touch with the child's view of the world. As I described its benefits, Clara wondered aloud whether such a class would work with parents who abuse their children.

At the time, we were both part-time counselors at Trailback Lodge, a residential program for disturbed adolescents, run by psychologist Bond Johnson. Dr. Johnson had purchased a house in Long Beach, California, to serve as a temporary residence for runaway adolescents. Paraprofessional Marilyn Johnson (no relation) was to be the housemother in residence.

Clara suggested we try a twelve-week class in "filial therapy" with a group of abusive parents in part of the house. We approached Dr. Elizabeth Kraft, the assistant director and, coincidentally, the wife of Dr. Arthur Kraft. The idea sounded good to her. Dr. Johnson's reaction was "I don't see why not." Within half an hour, with no bureaucratic delays or red tape, Cedar House was conceived.

Marilyn busied herself baking bread and cookies and delivering them to the neighbors, also letting them know of our plan in her gentle way. She was happy to fill her time while waiting for the runaway adolescents to appear. Little did we know that it was the child abuse program, not the adolescents, that would consume her energies in the years to come.

Clara and I approached those we knew from past days working for the Department of Public Social Services, the Probation Department, and Family Service of Long Beach. When we explained our plan, veteran social workers and probation officers expressed skepticism that we could get the people in their caseloads to attend a class, much less teach them anything. Some were reluctant to provide names, citing the right of confidentiality. It took several months to find two social workers willing to risk the referral of one client each. Their supervisor told us in private that they were sending us "the cream of the crap."

Since neither of the two clients had a phone (not unusual, we learned), we dropped in on them to invite them to the class. Somewhat baffled, they agreed to come. When Clara added a private client, we were ready to roll.

Our first group met on Monday morning, January 13, 1975, with the three mothers and we three staff members in one apartment and three children and a volunteer in the playroom across the hall. We felt an adventure about to begin.

This book, the chronicle of that adventure, has been years in the making, mostly in the processing of our experience. Clara has been the inspiring speaker of our team, taking the lead in our many presentations. I have been the writer, but until now my writing served primarily to produce papers to present at conferences. Many people urged us to write a book, and some offered to do the writing themselves. Dr. Morris Paulson of the UCLA Neuropsychiatric Institute told us it would be a "tragedy" to leave the story of Cedar House unwritten. Yet the years went by with only scattered observations on paper.

Finally the time came to reflect on our overall experience. Clara, Marilyn, Children's Counselor Pam Sheets, and I spent a few days together at the Quaker Center in Ben Lomond, California, to combine our store of memories and to assure the accuracy of that which I wrote. After I finished the first draft, Clara, Pam, Dr. Roland Summit, and I spent another day reviewing and reliving it.

The adults in the program included both offending and non-offending mothers, fathers, stepparents, other relatives, boyfriends, and girlfriends. Because the children were usually in the primary care of the mothers, some of whom were single parents, the majority of our adult clientele (perhaps 60 percent) consisted of women. Our writing reflects this at times. The description of the principles and treatment at Cedar House apply to both genders, however. The names of all the clients mentioned in the book have, of course, been changed to protect their privacy.

While I was privileged to be in the right place at the right time to be one of the founders of Cedar House, the vision for it and its nurturing in the early years came from Clara Lowry. My writing has brought us acceptance in some national and international forums, but much of what I have written started with her thoughts and her work. What she envisioned and brought into reality has touched more lives than we could ever have imagined. I offer my special thanks to her for the journey that we have shared, a journey that continues to this day.

Chapter 1

Our Founding Beliefs

In 1974, Clara and I were working part-time both at Trailback Lodge and at Family Service of Long Beach. We found ourselves treating overwhelmed parents struggling to maintain their households and dignity with little or no support from family, friends, or the community. We recognized the tensions that arose from the demands of raising children. We saw the results in frightened, sometimes bruised children. Somehow, somewhere, there needed to be a place for these families that offered more than an hourly session per week.

Thus it was that we began Cedar House. Our mission, as we envisioned it, was to prevent further child abuse among families in which injuries had already occurred and to avert abuse among potential abusers. Having witnessed the pain of parents and children when families were separated, we intended to help families stay together whenever possible while maintaining the bottom line of the protection of the child. We hoped to diminish the problem of child abuse by providing intensive outpatient therapy for the parents as well as support and a safe haven for those at risk from a rising rage level.

We founded Cedar House based on core beliefs shared by the two of us and our third partner, Marilyn Johnson. Some premises from which our work flowed included the following:

Parents do not want to hurt their children. In our experience working with families, we found most parents longed to be good parents. In a moment of rage, they had the urge to lash out hurtfully, but in calmer times the knowledge that they had or they could hurt their children was a source of enormous shame.

If one member of the family is hurting, all are hurting. We did not need to fix blame. We needed to deal with the pain in each member of the family and to understand how each one's consequent behavior contributed to the situation.

People have within them an urge to learn and grow if given fertile ground in which to do so. We set out to provide the nurturing setting to help remove that which had blocked their growth.

Problems can be solved. We chose not to become as helpless as our clients in dealing with apparently insurmountable problems. We did not know the answers in many situations, but we assumed there were some to be found.

Families have within them the answers to their problems. We could provide role models and suggestions of what worked for us and others we knew, but ultimately the clients would find their own way, possibly with solutions that would not have crossed our minds. We could afford to admit our own limitations, given our trust in the clients' abilities.

The clients can teach us. They would tell us what they needed if we would listen with a sensitive ear.

Abusive parents tend to be isolated from those around them. Part of our task was to reduce the isolation, to include them in a community, both in Cedar House itself and in the wider community whenever possible, thereby reducing the risk of abuse.

People are best helped by those who feel affection for them. We assumed the families' lives were sufficiently devoid of affection without having their worthlessness reaffirmed by us. This did not mean we relinquished the realistic awareness of risks to the children or the dysfunction of the parents, but we were prepared to find them likable.

Children are people with value and problems in their own right. This may seem a self-evident statement, but it was amazing how often children were overlooked in programs at the time. They were supposed to be all right, previous abuse notwithstanding, once the parents improved, but they had their own traumatic experiences to deal with.

Child abuse, a community problem, requires a coordinated community solution. We knew there was no way we and the families could solve their multiple problems without the resources and the support of many other programs, agencies, and individuals, working in concert. This was no place for turf wars.

This is what we had in mind when we began. We found these premises to be sound in our years of work with abusive families. In the following pages we will elaborate on how our assumptions influenced the actions we took as Cedar House evolved and how our experiences may prove useful to others dealing with similar problems.

Chapter 2

Staffing

No one alone is wise enough or emotionally strong enough to meet all the needs of distressed families. Those planning to work with child abuse cases need to build up a network and a support system for themselves as well as for the clients.

Ideally the work is done in a team with complementary skills and training. Since many fields touch upon the lives of abused children, almost any skill can be utilized for their benefit. We started with two social workers and two paraprofessionals, and we soon brought in a consulting psychiatrist and a volunteer psychologist. In later years, with more funding, the Cedar House staff included psychologists; educators; marriage, family, and child counselors; a recreation therapist; an administrator as executive director; and clerical staff. Consultants included a psychiatrist, a pediatrician, a dentist, and an occupational therapist. We often longed for a staff nurse, a consulting lawyer (who was added after our time), and a financial expert to consult with clients on budgeting.

Most important of all, the staff must have a working relationship of trust in each other, to avoid modeling the fragmentation that so many of these families had experienced. In our case, Clara, Marilyn Johnson, paraprofessional Pam Sheets (the children's counselor), and I chose to work closely together, partly to protect ourselves from burnout but mostly out of a conviction that providing a broader range of staff members was more effective for the families.

Clara, whose background included public social service and probation, was the one with the vision. While we did not initially think of ourselves in a hierarchical structure, she was the program director and group leader, with a strong sense of empathy, an equally strong sense of humor, and a playful side that often saved our sanity. She set the tone of total acceptance of the clients, along with firm expectations and limits. She demanded a great deal of herself and somehow inspired the rest of us to do the same, staff and clients alike.

Marilyn, the resident paraprofessional, was our crisis worker. Small in stature and unassuming in manner, with a background of community organization in rural Minnesota, she was magnificent at mothering, knowledgeable about community resources, and skilled at calming those who were out of control. She was also able to set a firm limit on those who would abuse her kindness. She could call the sour milk in a baby's bottle to the mother's attention, demonstrate how to clean the bottle, and substitute fresh milk—all without putting the mother on the defensive. When we were interviewed by local journalist Frank Anderson, he remarked that at the heart of every dynamic program he found a paraprofessional. In our program, that was Marilyn.

I brought to Cedar House a background in public social services, an empathy for a child's position in an adult world, and a sense of how the child perceives that world. Yet as a mother, I could also identify with the parents and their struggles. As such, I served as the advocate for the child in the adult groups. Clara described me as "gentle, slower to react than the rest of us, more thoughtful, providing a corrective balance to our reactive, intuitive work."

Soon after our first group began, we started a search for funds to pay a childcare worker. Through a government program known as the California Employment Training Act (CETA), we hired Pam Sheets, a young woman with a warmly welcoming voice and a remarkable capacity to give of herself. Her ability to empathize with and enjoy young children and to relate to the parents as well proved to be invaluable. Pam taught me the art of welcoming people at the front door. "Hi, Jimmy! I'm glad to see you!" she would say, and there was no question that she meant it. Little Jimmy perked up even before he reached the playroom.

In the beginning Cedar House did not have the funds to hire many professionals. Clara and I, with our masters degrees, were paid part-time, though we both worked more hours than we were paid for. The paraprofessionals, Marilyn and Pam, received training on the job, but Clara and I learned a great deal from them as well.

Somehow, the combination of the four of us, along with a legion of unpaid consultants and volunteers, teachers, administrators, and supporters plus a few staff members added in later years, produced what was later chosen as the model child abuse program for Los Angeles County.

I learned a lot from our close teamwork. For example, a mother whom I shall call Ann bothered me because of her harsh treatment of her daughter and her hard manner. Marilyn, however, had developed a caring relationship with her. Thanks to our trust in each other, I assumed there must be something in Ann that I had not yet discovered, for I knew Marilyn to be realistic as well as empathetic. I stayed out of the way.

Then one day I got it. As Marilyn and Ann talked at the table, I suddenly caught the hurt behind Ann's hardened manner. From then on, I could deal with her with far more compassion, even as I advocated for her child's right to protection. Without my respect for Marilyn's perceptions, I doubt that I could ever have approached Ann with any real liking.

When Pam accompanied a family to their intake interview in another agency, she was appalled to hear the two interviewers in conflict, contradicting each other and unable to hide their annoyance. The conflict was left hanging. In such a case, when the staff members do not show respect for each other, the concept of a team can be counterproductive.

It is not always necessary for conflicts to be unseen, however. One morning, before a group session, Clara and Pam had a disagreement. Clara, who was not present when a crisis arose the previous day, felt strongly that it should have been handled differently. Pam asserted that she had done the best she knew how under the circumstances. Feelings ran high.

As they argued, the group members arrived one by one and silently took their places at the table, witnessing the scene. Their anxiety was palpable. Clara and Pam, deep into the argument, made no attempt to dampen the discussion. In time, however, Clara acknowledged that Pam was acting out of her concern for the family, and Pam commented that she would handle a similar situation differently in the future. The two of them hugged and turned their attention to the group.

Though unplanned, this was one of the more therapeutic moments in our work. The mothers' relief was as apparent as had been their anxiety. Several group members admitted they had expected the argument to end in blows, for this had been their experience with conflicts in the past. One mother commented, "In any arguments that I've known, people go around and around in a circle and go nowhere. You two went around and around and then exited." We could have talked endlessly about how to deal with conflict, but the demonstration proved far more meaningful.

It took time, of course, for us to become so familiar with each others' working styles that our thoughts and actions blended effortlessly together. The fact that none of the four of us had particular ambitions for our own career enhancement probably kept problems of ego in check.

We believe strongly that any effective treatment team can only be based on mutual respect for each other and the clients and on a compatibility among the staff in their perception of those served. When tensions arise among staff members, they must be dealt with and laid to rest to avoid diverting staff energy from the program's purpose of serving the needs of clients.

When it works, the rewards are limitless.

Chapter 3

The Setting

The physical setting in which a program is housed sends off many cues to those who enter. At Cedar House, where we expected to serve families with high levels of fear and mistrust, we were concerned from the start that a family's first impression be inviting rather than intimidating. We anticipated that some of the clients had been demoralized in institutional settings when their children were removed from them. Here we wanted to send signals of safety and welcome, stability and trustworthiness. We wanted the atmosphere to be comfortable, homey, and aesthetically pleasing. We did not want a family's first view of the program to be the barrier of a front desk with a receptionist. When clients entered our door, they were greeted by staff members, calling ourselves by our first names, and with no furniture between us. Desks and paperwork stayed out of sight.

The name "Cedar House" came from our location, which was then on Cedar Avenue in the heart of Long Beach. We chose the name for its connotations of shelter and stability embodied in the image of a tree.

A professional decorator had furnished the rooms with an emphasis on comfort. The living room provided a large couch with coves to sink into and chairs of differing sizes. The dining room, bright and cheery with its yellow curtains and live plants by the sunlit windows, contained built-in cupboards that reminded community visitors of their grandmothers' homes. A local government official remarked that he had always wondered what was in the overhead cupboards at his grandmother's house. We gave him permission to peek into our cupboards, to his delight and satisfaction.

We believed it made sense to provide a homelike setting if we hoped to have the parents carry new skills and attitudes into their own homes. To that end, Marilyn worked with mothers in the kitchen to show them how to clean bottles or make chicken soup, cinnamon rolls, or playdough. We learned that some of the parents had never experienced sharing around a dining room table. Some were moved by the new experience, while others took time to get comfortable sitting so close to other people. The table itself, quite ordinary in its rectangular shape, became meaningful to the group members. Often we spoke of bringing a problem "to the table" for discussion. As the groups met there, helping themselves to whatever food was served and comparing their hurts and joys, we discussed what memories such sharing in their own homes could bring to their children and others in their families.

The children were separated from their parents by a small entryway between the two apartments. At the intake and again at the family's first group meeting, we showed the child where the parents sat before inviting him or her into the playroom. The decorator had done a more eye-jolting treatment of the children's room, which was carpeted with a multicolor, flashy pattern of children's games. This provided more soundproofing than the wood floor it covered. It also camouflaged the crayons of many colors that fell. When one of those crayons fell through the vent into the furnace below, the resulting stench overpowered even the smell of soiled pants.

The playroom contained a child-size table and chairs, beanbag chairs, toys galore, and a mural depicting monkeys and giraffes, which was painted by a volunteer. We had the benefit of an entire apartment for the children, including a large undivided living/dining room, a kitchen, a bathroom, and a small back room. During free play the children roamed freely in the large room, playing with the toys or drawing at the table. The kitchen served, like that on the adult side, to introduce the children to the smells and tastes of activities such as baking cookies and making homemade craft dough. The small back room served for children who were out of control and needed containment.

In that room, too, Pam dealt with children who simply could not tolerate open spaces, those who became anxious in the large room. During a trip to a nearby playground, one child ran aimlessly in all directions in a state of high anxiety, heedless of our efforts to get his attention. He and others like him had lived confined lives in small apartments or had been shut in closets as punishment. Unfamiliar with open space, they experienced large areas as threatening to their sense of safety. At Cedar House they sometimes needed the smaller room.

Potty time in the bathroom provided a natural setting for taking an unobtrusive look at the small children's bodies to check for bruises or signs of abuse. The bathtub served for the occasional child who severely soiled his or her pants and also helped children who had been scalded in hot bath water. A two-year-old boy whose feet had been burned climbed in and out of the empty tub, saying, "hot, hot, hot, hot," reenacting the traumatic experience in the presence of an understanding adult.

I once heard a therapist remark that a child feels more comfortable if he or she sees a toy or two out of place, not in perfect order. Where possible, I recommend setting aside at least one room for children with no desks, signaling that this space is entirely for them, a place to play, not where the adults work. Elsewhere in the setting there are enough cues that this is a place set up by and for adults, but in this room they are the important ones. While some therapists prefer to bring out toys one at a time for a defined purpose, I prefer to have the room set up with toys from which the child may choose, giving me more cues to what is on the child's mind rather than mine. A few children may want to handle every toy in the first session, but they soon settle on what they need to express themselves. This preference for accessible or specified toys may reflect the degree to which a therapist needs a sense of control.

Some who visited Cedar House questioned whether it was appropriate to have such a nicely furnished setting for people of poverty, who were presumed to live in and be more comfortable in shabbier surroundings. We found, however, that the clients were not so different from the rest of us. Some looked forward each week to spending time in a pretty place. I came to believe that the assumption of a preference for shabbiness was simply another example of blaming the victim.

A mother whose apartment crawled with cockroaches brought her boyfriend to our first open house. I overheard her enthusiastic comment as they mounted the front steps, "See, this is the house I've been telling you about!" She did not comment on those of us who had transported her, answered her calls, looked after her children, and seen her through many a crisis. She wanted to show him the house.

We find our former clients and volunteers still nostalgic about the house, though many years have passed. Recently, Clara and I met with a woman we had served nearly twenty years ago. She was moving out of town but wanted first to tell us what Cedar House had meant to her. Among other things, she stressed that the "homey" setting made it possible to open up because "it was like being in my living room." Another client who has stayed in touch remarked that it was important to her to be able to see the entire length of the house. "There were no closed doors. In institutional buildings, there were all those closed doors, and some of us wondered if there could be policemen with handcuffs lurking behind them."

As for me, I found that the setting made a subtle difference in the way I worked as a professional. Sitting at the dining room table, sipping coffee together, invariably reduces distance. The inviting and comfortable environment set the tone for all of us, clients and staff alike.

While it is unusual to run an agency in a house setting, it is by no means unheard of. Children's Home Society, Children's Institute International, and Children's Bureau of Los Angeles have used houses for services to families. Options Family Center in Covina, California, has maintained a treatment program in a house for many years. Executive Director Cliff Marcussen is so sold on the concept of a residential setting that when the agency needed to expand, they purchased two more houses, one in Covina and one in San Gabriel.

For some, the temptation is to look for a larger space in one building, which usually means a more institutional setting. Even Cedar House, which burned down well after our time, is now located in an office building with more rooms for services but lacking the residential tone.

Ultimately, of course, the trust that evolves between the therapist and the adult or child is what makes the difference in how the therapy proceeds. In our experience, however, the setting as I have described it enhances the development of trust, as it signals a welcome and safety for those who enter.

Chapter 4

Team Intakes

The use of the entire staff for intakes turned out to be one of the program's more fortuitous innovations. Entering the house for the first time required a great deal of courage from these parents. As identified child abusers, they were ashamed, demoralized, and in many cases, depressed.

As already noted, we were concerned that their first view of us send a message of welcome with no barriers. We moved toward them when they entered. We showed them the playroom, and the children had their choice of staying there with Pam or remaining by the parents. We offered them something, usually a cup of coffee, perhaps juice if the children stayed with us, and we gathered at the dining room table rather than by a desk. Here they met all or most of the staff. Often the table was crowded, particularly as the staff grew larger and when a social worker or probation officer accompanied the family to the intake.

While we had our chance to evaluate the family members, they also had a chance to size us up. The parents could see for themselves who would be with their children, a matter of high anxiety for some. We watched for the connections that developed as we talked. It became clear in the first meeting who would be the most appropriate staff person to work with each one in the family.

The benefits of this system exceeded our expectations. Our trust in each other turned out to be contagious to the newcomers. While some questioned whether a roomful of people would be threatening to newcomers, we found that they soon opened up in an atmosphere of easy laughter and shared concern. Our comments among ourselves somehow helped the clients become a sharing part of the scene. Even depressed and withdrawn clients responded to someone in the room sooner or later. That staff member was the most likely to become the individual's primary connection to Cedar House—not necessarily as the therapist but as the emotional supporter for the work to follow.

Our clientele included many people prone to crises. This could be draining, especially when crisis calls overlapped. When one of us needed time off for vacations or mental health days, this was not a major problem for our clients because of our staff intakes. The families had some familiarity with everyone on the staff, and the staff had some familiarity with each client. When parents called or dropped in, they had a broad range of support to draw on, bolstered by the trust they had witnessed among us. On one occasion a distraught man came to the door and asked for Marilyn. Told that Marilyn was not available, he looked at Clara, said, "I guess you'll have to do," and drew up a chair.

Many of our clients had learned in their families of origin to keep secrets or to play family members against each other. "You're the only one I would tell this to," they might say, or "I don't want anyone else to know." We made it clear that what was shared with one was shared with the therapeutic team. We assured them of confidentiality outside of Cedar House, short of our responsibility to report abuse, but within the program we did not keep secrets. The staff intakes set the tone to ensure that the treatment the families received did not prove as fragmented as their experiences in their own families and, frequently, in the government system. Ultimately this added to the parents' sense of security, for in a time of crisis they did not need to start from square one with the available staff person.

Nor did we keep it a secret from them that this was a child abuse treatment program and that we would be looking at the children's bodies. (Toilet needs, playing in the sprinkler with shirts off, and the occasional child who required a bath offered natural opportunities for this.) We always assured the parents that we assumed they were even more concerned than we were that their children be safe. Parental resistance lowered remarkably when we focused on abuse as a *human* problem, rather than as *their* problem. Clara often said, "We all have it in us to abuse those we love, some with our mouths, some with our fists. Let's look at how it is we do that."

Staff intakes brought more minds to bear on the families' problems, which were usually myriad. Demoralized as they were, the parents' problem-solving skills had become constricted, leaving them with a hopeless view of their situation. Almost invariably, someone at the table had an idea of how to proceed toward overcoming what had seemed to the parent to be an insurmountable obstacle. Clara was good at providing the parent with words to set limits with an impossible relative, or to deal with those in the system. I came up with approaches to use with an acting-out child. With her knowledge of community resources, Marilyn knew where to go for help with the utility bills, housing, drug or alcohol programs, job training, need for groceries, or whatever need they mentioned. Sometimes we brought the telephone to the table to start the process on the spot.

Clara generally took the lead in exploring family dynamics and social supports, but we all took part. While not asking for details, we explored the age of the client's earliest memories to determine the likelihood of the parent's ability to identify with a young child's experience. We often asked, "Who has loved you?" and noted whether the parent responded with a bleak "Nobody," a ready reply with warmth ("My grandmother!"), a long pause before naming someone, or an assurance of a happy childhood, given the lie by their manner. Frequently the question alone elicited tears. The answers to this simple query gave us clues to the degree of the client's needs to be nurtured, to grieve past losses, to overcome denial, and to grapple with repressed material.

We noted to what degree the adult and the child took on, rejected, or projected blame for the abuse that had occurred. We explored what people did when they were angry. Clara sometimes put forth trial balloons, posing a possibly touchy subject and then moving back as needed. "Would you say you are a controlling kind of parent?" she might say. If the parent reacted defensively, she would acknowledge the need to have some parental control while we all made a mental note to explore control issues in the course of treatment.

We listened for the language that clients used. Many a parent reported, "I didn't hit him. I just popped him one," or "swatted," or "slapped," or "smacked." The child had indeed been hit, but the parent's urge was to trivialize the incident. We also listened for words that indicated resentment of the child, abuse, or neglect in the parent's past:

- "He *always* does that to me!"
- "He's awkward" or "clumsy."
- "He's bad" or "mean" or "evil."
- "He bruises easily."
- "He *never* sleeps."
- "He's impossible."
- "He's the boss."
- "I got hit. Why not them?"
- "I was hit, but I deserved it."
- "I raised my brothers and sisters."

We learned to ask at intakes whether the mother had been molested as a child. Many replied, "How did you know?"

If the child had stayed with us, Pam joined us long enough for the families to get comfortable and then invited the children to the playroom, with the permission of the parents. By this time we all had some sense of how the family functioned, and they had some sense of how we operated. We had to develop a finely tuned sensitivity to those who were terrified of the separation from their children, experiencing it as another effort to take their babies away from them or, in some cases, fearing what the children might say and how we would react.

We looked upon the intake as the beginning of treatment for the family. With this population it could not be routine, for those who went away feeling no more hope than when they came were not likely to return.

While team intakes are effective and more rewarding for both clients and staff, we have seldom seen them elsewhere, possibly because the thought has not crossed most administrators' minds. Obviously it would be unworkable for a very large staff to cram into one room for an intake, and a conference room would not be the ideal setting to put a nervous client at ease. It should be possible, however, for those programs treating child abuse to arrange for clients to meet at least two or preferably three compatible staff members at the time of intake and for some kind of interaction to continue with a miniteam. The treatment would be strengthened by more eyes to see and more minds to focus on the problems.

A director of a clinic once agonized with me over the fact that a teenager in the program had committed suicide while her therapist was on vacation. The director concluded, "It couldn't be helped. The therapist needed a vacation." Possibly, but could it have been prevented if the therapist and the teenager had had more backup? It occurred to me that we had never lost a client during our time at Cedar House, though we worked with a high number of violent and suicidal people. Perhaps we were lucky.

Chapter 5

The Parents

The families in Cedar House were those in which child abuse (physical, sexual, emotional, or potential) or neglect was the presenting problem and in which the children included preadolescents who were in the home or were due to come home soon from placement. Some of the parents were court-ordered to attend therapy. They were referred by a wide variety of agencies, while some were self-referred. We screened out families with adolescents where there were no younger children, as well as those who lived too far away to be reached in times of crisis. Motivated and articulate families who could be treated in more traditional settings were referred elsewhere, if the reported abuse was not severe. After two years of struggling to treat parents' suffering from psychoses, we reluctantly decided to screen them out as well, given the increasing demand for out services. We hoped to see another program develop specifically for families with parents who suffer from mental illness. Both the adults and the children in these families desperately need a haven.

Cedar House parents came from all walks of life, all races, classes, and psychiatric diagnoses. They reflected the ethnic composition of Long Beach, a multiethnic city. Caucasians, English-speaking Latinos, African Americans, Pacific Islanders, Native Americans, and a few Asians found their way to our door.

Parents who hurt their children impressed us as particularly needy people. Among the mothers, many were oldest daughters who were left in charge of younger siblings at a very early age, acting as parents before they were parented. They boasted, "I've been taking care of kids since I was seven years old." Many still functioned as emotionally dependent children while trying to raise their own children. At Cedar House they leaned on the staff and volunteers until they found a more stable base on which to forge their independence.

Most, if not all, shared a history of abuse, though not always physical abuse. The common denominator appeared to be a sense of abandonment, whether experienced through a parent's actual absence or through emotional unavailability. Many had indeed experienced physical abuse as children. One of our more startling findings was the number of mothers of abused and neglected children who reported having been sexually abused at an early age, usually before age twelve, and by one or more close relatives or trusted friends. We estimated the rate of such reports to be about 90 percent, for the exceptions were rare.

In a group of six mothers, all six reported experiences of molestation. In another group of eight, seven reported molestation by a father, stepfather, or uncle. The eighth mother later remembered a sexual incident with her stepfather when she inadvertently touched his penis as they shared the same bed—hardly an abusive situation, for he was asleep, but at age four it had frightened her deeply.

These same young mothers, some of whom came to hate and fear men, were now raising sons. In the groups we asked how the mothers bathed their tiny sons' penises. One mother admitted to being unable to look at her sons from the neck down. (It was her three-year-old son who exposed his penis in the playroom, holding it up and calling out, "Dukie! Dukie!"—pleading for someone to look. He evidently feared for its very existence if no one else acknowledged it.) Most mothers reported discomfort or even revulsion at the sight of a small boy's penis. One mother was preoccupied with cleaning her son's penis to an excessive degree.

Some of the parents described themselves as "emotionally dead." In retrospect, when more hopeful times came, they saw themselves as having been "dormant," waiting for a bit of sun before putting forth a tentative bud. There was a profound emptiness in their lives, an assumption in their basic being that no one cared for them, that no one could care for them, that they were so bad that they were not entitled to be cared for. They did not know where they belonged. Most of them, having received considerable punishment and abuse as they grew up, viewed themselves as deserving of punishment. It

followed that they often found ways to punish themselves, sometimes by striking out at the child who reminded them of themselves—the "bad" self.

So as not to experience the void, Cedar House families tried to
fill their emptiness in various ways: eating, sex, becoming pregnant,
fighting, keeping in a constant state of turmoil and anger. If I am
angry, I am something. To paraphrase Descartes: "I feel; therefore I
am." If I cease to be angry (or pregnant or whatever), I become
emotionally dead. I cease to be.

Thus these families frequently had a need to be embroiled in
crisis. If they did not have enough turmoil in their lives, they would
become involved in fights on behalf of their neighbors. If their lives
were running smoothly, they became anxious: "This can't last
because I don't deserve it. When will the next blow fall?" They
could not tolerate a moment of quiet, for that risked evoking
despair. To relieve the anxiety, they would provoke a crisis. They
led lives punctuated by accidents or sickness, fights, suicide attempts,
sudden separations, or financial dilemmas. ("There's no milk for the
baby, and I don't have any money.") They were crisis-prone.

At the same time, the parents were quick to see where others had
wronged them. Since they expected bad things to happen to them,
they were sensitized to the wrongs in their lives. If a glass was half
full, they would see it as not only half empty but completely empty.
It was exceedingly difficult for a spouse or a child to please them.
Having had little opportunity to be children themselves, they expected
their own children to be instant adults. They frequently looked to
their children for care ("Sammy, bring me a cup of coffee!") without being aware that the child needed care. Needy themselves, they
were unable to see the needs of another. Often they became enraged
when the child wanted something from them instead of serving to
fill their void.

Working with people referred for child abuse, we saw a great
deal of both rage and depression. At times when the rage was
dormant, the parent often sank into depression. Given their emptiness and their assumption of their own unworthiness, depressed
parents were usually unable to reach out for help, particularly in the
times when they most needed it. The families became isolated from
the world around them, for they saw no hope in reaching out to

others. Thus, if we wanted to reach them, it was necessary to model the reaching out.

Trust was a major issue, which was no surprise given their life histories. With some who had never known anyone they could count on, we knew we could not expect them to trust us right away. Why should they? Some adults required a year or longer with us before they could risk more than the most superficial relationship. Most found it difficult to reach out for help, thus narrowing the chances of developing a support system. Some sought help relentlessly, driving their friends away and confirming in their minds that no one was to be trusted.

Ambivalence was common. Raised with uncertainty regarding parental love ("I think they love me but I'm not sure"), the parents were unable to take a confident step in any direction. As adults they had difficulty making decisions and often acted on impulse without thinking a matter through.

Parents at Cedar House often showed a remarkable lack of judgment regarding what was appropriate for small children. The parent's choice of a toy (a cola bottle), a recreation (X-rated movies), or a punishment (a two-year-old child expected to sit in the corner for an hour) invariably reflected the parent's own background. "Common sense" is not so common as we would like to think. It appears to require grounding in early guidelines.

Sometimes the parents, particularly in the neglect situations, were remarkably ignorant of the most basic child care. They were unaware of the need to clean a baby's bottle between feedings or to medicate a diaper rash. Some benefited from step-by-step instructions on how to care for a baby. Others were too depressed to follow through on such instructions. Some appeared to use up their emotional energy in the suppression of their rage. If they believed that engaging with others carried the risk of feeling something intolerable, their withdrawal from their babies could be seen as both self-protective and a way to avoid lashing out and doing harm.

Some of the parents had vivid, usually bitter, childhood memories. Others could remember nothing, or almost nothing, before the age of ten or twelve. While both groups had a high degree of rage, the parents lacking their childhood memories tended to be the more dysfunctional and isolated group. They had an almost total inability to empathize with a child, for they had not experienced the child part of themselves. It did no good to say, "Do you remember what it felt like when . . . ?" They did not. They had no way to know what it felt like to be six until they regained those early memories and the child part of themselves.

Along the same lines, many of the parents were unable to play and enjoy themselves when they first came to Cedar House. They were not permitted to play as children, and it was very difficult for them to allow their children to play. Fortunately, several staff members had a flair for playful exchanges which opened the door for others to join in.

Never underestimate the human spirit. One of the joys of the work at Cedar House was to see the emerging playfulness of those who arrived looking emotionally flat. There was fun in these abusive parents, but that, too, had been dormant.

Chapter 6

Group Therapy with Parents

Given our assumption that those who abused children tended to be socially isolated, we formed the program around groups, not only to serve greater numbers, but more important, to provide a milieu in which the members could develop social skills.

Because we wanted no insurmountable impediments for families with children at risk, we arranged transportation—rides with staff members, volunteers, or each other—for some who found it difficult to come. We provided coffee and food, doughnuts at first, but as we noticed the clients' eating disorders, we turned to healthier fare such as fruit or carrot sticks. The daytime groups met around the dining room table, while evening groups met in the living room with lit candles, one of Marilyn's touches.

After our first group, a twelve-week "filial therapy class" (see Chapter 17), we did not follow a structured design, but we stayed alert for themes in the material the participants brought. If a parent expressed fury with a mate, a child, or the system, we directed the discussion to how various group members handled their anger, what triggered them, and what they could do to discharge the anger without hurting somebody. A mother's depressed demeanor prompted discussions of the emptiness that so many felt in their lives, which of their actions were attempts to fill that void, and what it would take to fill it. A complaint of a child's impossible behavior was an opening for (1) validating the parent who found raising a child a difficult task; (2) exploring the parent's memories, if any, of that time in his or her own childhood; (3) attempting to bring that inner child in touch with the current child, and then, after the inner child work; (4) a discussion of expected child development and how to handle the normal problems of that age.* When someone reported the theft of food stamps or an imminent eviction, we focused on legal and community resources, concrete problem-solving, and sometimes mutual assistance among the group members.

We listened to the parents' woes, but we also made a point of discussing each child before the group ended. In the early sessions, few group members thought to mention their children. We set out to bring the little ones to their awareness, but it was not always easy.

We did not scold parents for spanking their children, but bearing in mind that we were working with an abusive population that had difficulty maintaining control, we never gave them permission to spank. We heard some therapists argue for teaching *how* to spank—with the open hand on the butt, no more than twice—but we heard too many parents report that once they started hitting, they found it too hard to stop, just as an alcoholic cannot stop with one drink. We believed strongly (and still do) in helping parents find more effective methods of discipline than spanking.

Our first groups consisted primarily of mothers, mostly because we met in the mornings. Most of the women were eager to tell their own stories to anyone who would listen and some who would not. Some did verbal battle, whether or not they had an adversary. Some bombarded us with a wall of words, sometimes in a monotone. Others were initially silent and uncomfortable. We were gentle with the latter, occasionally opening the door for them to speak, but never pushing for a response.

Sandy, a recluse who lived behind drawn shades with her three-year-old daughter, was one who found it difficult at first to speak. Her social worker did not believe she would come, but following a home visit by Clara and Marilyn, she showed up. She had to arrive earlier than the other group members, for she could not bear to enter a room full of people. In group she frequently stared into space. We did not insist that Sandy join in the discussion, but in her own time she told her story of past abuse and suicide attempts. She became a regular attender.

---

*We did not use the term "inner child" at the time, but, making use of Transaction Analysis's concept of the Parent-Adult-Child, we often spoke of the "child within."

Clara, Marilyn, and I, co-leaders, chose to start our first group on Monday mornings to get the families' week started with a place to go. The "Monday group" consisted mostly of women with high rage levels, few parenting or social skills, chaotic lives, and sometimes litter-strewn homes. In time a few fathers, stepfathers, and boyfriends joined us, but the group continued primarily as a mothers' group. Since none of them led lives of routine, Marilyn phoned those with telephones early on Monday mornings to be sure they were awake in time. "Are you sitting up?" she would ask. "Are your feet on the floor?"

It took some doing to get this unlikely combination of isolates to start responding as a functional group. Clara, however, kept acting as though they were, and in time, true to the theory of self-fulfilling prophecies, they became so. Their cohesion was apparent the time that Esther's baby was kidnapped.

Esther was a young Navy wife whose husband was at sea. She had nothing good to say of her mother or the rest of her large family. Her two-year-old son was in foster care, but Esther was permitted to have him on weekends, returning him to his foster home after our Monday group.

One morning, arriving without the boy, Esther reported that he was sick but that her mother would return him to the foster home. We were uneasy. At our urging, Esther reluctantly phoned home and spoke with her mother, her end of the conversation adding to our uneasiness. A volunteer drove her home immediately to see to the return of the child, but the grandmother and child were gone by the time they arrived. The missing pair did not show up at the foster home.

We called the police. Days went by with no word. Esther denied any knowledge of where they were, but the other group members were not convinced. They were in fact furious.

We called an emergency meeting to deal with the situation. Esther sat with her head down, still denying any involvement, but looking at no one. Sandy, the recluse, came alive, almost lunging across the table as she shouted, "You do, too, know where he is! You're lying! You arranged for this to happen!"

The grandmother and the boy were eventually located in Las Vegas and returned to Long Beach. The child was hospitalized briefly for dehydration and placed in a different foster home. In group Esther told of her decision to give him up for adoption and added that she had falsely told her mother the boy was placed in another city. The group cheered. Those who had been so furious with her for lying were now cheering her for lying, but they had coalesced out of concern for someone outside of themselves, a child.

When I noted that the group supported lies that served a purpose of safety and survival, Esther gulped and owned for the first time that sometimes she lied. It was a memorable moment.

The group was also helpful in the case of Helen. Feisty, full of tales of the crises in her life, swearing as readily as breathing, she told us more than we wanted to know of her private life. (We chuckled as we remembered her social worker's earlier concerns about confidentiality.) Helen's six-year-old daughter had been in foster care for more than two years.* For weeks she asserted her determination to get her daughter back despite the alleged hostility of the social worker. Group members were sympathetic until we invited the social worker to the group to outline what was expected of Helen. When the group learned that Helen had not visited her daughter for many months, though the foster home was local, their mood changed dramatically, providing the social worker with an instant group of indignant allies. Eventually the child was put up for adoption against Helen's spoken wishes, but with the group's, and our, blessing.

From time to time we invited people from the community to attend a group meeting, always with the permission of the group. If we wanted those who isolated themselves to become more a part of the larger society, we reasoned, we needed to put them in touch with the community and vice versa. Sometimes those invited served a need to solve a specific problem. Sometimes they came to educate. On one occasion a dentist came to examine teeth.

We had discovered that some of the mothers had never seen a dentist. Some, not surprisingly, had real dental problems. A local dentist agreed to examine the teeth of the children and of the mothers during a group session.

The mothers had no problem allowing him to look at their children's teeth, but when it came to their own, terror reigned. We explained that

---

*California law has since changed to prevent such long-term placements.

he planned only to look, not to do any work on them at the time, but the fear in the air remained palpable. Margaret, a mother who generally dealt with problems by trying to laugh them off, literally clutched her chair, asserting, "I'm not going in there! I won't!" It took much persuasion by the group members who had already braved the experience before Margaret allowed the dentist to examine her teeth.

Almost all of these mothers had been sexually molested, some with early experiences of oral sex. We realized the idea of dental work was bad enough, but what terrified them the most was having someone, particularly a man, invade their mouths—or any cavity of their bodies, for that matter.

At the end of their first twelve weeks, celebrating the completion of the "filial therapy class," the Monday group gave a party, the mothers serving as hosts to their social workers, probation officers, relatives, boyfriends, or whomever they chose to invite. They helped bake cookies for the event, a first experience for some. Social workers and probation officers came and were given a tour of the house by their clients. For the duration of the morning, the mothers were the hosts, a role that drew them out of the one-down position. Even Helen, who could not restrain herself from a loud "Oh f---!" when she broke the coffeepot, glowed the rest of the time. To our amazement, Sandy, the former recluse, appointed herself to greet those arriving at the door! It was a glorious day.

Our second group tended to consist of higher-functioning mothers: a Navy wife who called after she had the urge to "mop up the floor" with her small daughter while her husband was at sea (but, we noted, she stopped herself); a thoughtful prostitute exploring how and even whether to raise her young son; a woman married to an alcoholic and carrying two jobs while raising three boys; a young mother who had been molested for years by her father but had the courage in her teens to confront him and put a stop to it; and others. Most demonstrated more ego strength than those in the Monday group.

While these participants required less effort on our part to engage them in the group and to sustain attendance, their histories of abuse were also horrifying. Most of them retained their early memories, however. In at least one case the parent did not suffer abuse as a child but suffered traumatic assaults as an adult. We still had to treat post-traumatic stress in this clientele, but we did not have to work as hard to form the group.

When a retired psychologist, Dr. Larry Hanna, volunteered his time, he and Clara co-led an evening couples' group, modeling a healthy relationship between a man and a woman. Some of the couples were married; some were not. All of those in couples' group were also involved in other therapy at Cedar House, whether mothers' or fathers' group, individual, or marital counseling. (A visiting therapist noted that we provided "saturation therapy.") Bringing the partners with all their volatile issues into a single group made it more complicated than the other groups, for sexual temptations ran rampant in this gathering of people with confused boundaries. Clara and Larry became aware of shifting loyalties and some swapping of partners.

Some who also attended mothers' groups were seen in a different light in the couples' group. It became obvious, for instance, that one was constantly on the lookout for someone other than her husband, an observation overlooked in the mothers' group. Clara recently mused that if she had such a group to do again, she would begin by establishing a firm rule, rather than waiting to put out fires as they arose. "You may find yourselves tempted by the attractions of those of the opposite sex," she would say, "but that is not what we are here for!" Whether such an admonition would lead the couples to be more secretive about their liaisons, we will never know.

Larry, unflappable, confrontive yet loving, generally became the objective father figure while Clara served as the more emotional mother figure. The respect between the two of them made it possible for them to agree or disagree openly in front of the group, usually with humor, always with affection. It was new to many in the group to be with a man and woman who could care about each other and yet tolerate disagreement.

Occasionally the group shared potlucks, which proved to be lessons in social skills. Few knew how to cook. One couple brought wine, though alcohol was not permitted in the Cedar House setting. Large families might show up with no food. Clara and Larry learned that the potlucks required considerable planning if they hoped to have a decent meal. Cedar House quickly added a homemaking class to its schedule.

One night, addressing a man who had appeared to be devoid of emotion until that time, Clara asked the inevitable question, "Who has really loved you?" The man began to cry. His response became a touchstone for the entire group, for it opened up for all of them, fathers included, the pain that most of them shared. They recognized then how hard it was for them to love their children, after having received so little love themselves.

One of the men, Rick, was hard-headed, short but husky, and full of resentment toward women. While the others were more likely to become angry with Larry's comments, Rick had a visceral reaction to Clara. "I would be able to talk," he would say meaningfully, "if a certain person was not in the room!" He loved to sing wherever he happened to be and whenever the mood came over him. He had a good voice with considerable volume, appropriate for a stage presentation, overpowering in the smaller setting of Cedar House. Clara questioned whether it was always agreeable to neighbors or people on the street when Rick chose to sing at full volume on a whim. Rick reacted—as usual—in anger.

Rick lived with a woman and her three-year-old daughter, who were referred to Cedar House after he allegedly broke the child's arm. He denied the charge, but in time he got word that the police were coming to arrest him. Rick may have resented that certain person, but Clara was the one he called when he was in need. She was with him when the police arrived.

Rick served time in prison before returning to Cedar House. We welcomed him back and heard from him for several years thereafter. More than once he brought his keyboard instrument and voice to entertain at our functions.

In time, when funding permitted a larger staff, we added another afternoon mothers' group and an evening men's group under the leadership of our first male therapist, Lynn Seiser, a marriage, family, and child counselor. This group, consisting of fathers, stepfathers, and boyfriends, differed in that there was no concurrent children's group, nor did Lynn have a cotherapist. After twenty intervening years of feminist thought, we recognize that the women, even those who had been the abusers, were expected to be caretakers of their children during the men's meetings while the same expectation did not apply to the men when the mothers met. Partly due to the limitations of staff time but probably also due to our mindset, we did not treat child care for the fathers' group as thoughtfully as we did for the mothers' groups.

Noting the self-absorption of the men who attended, Lynn sought to bring each one to an awareness of the inner child, to connect them with their children's needs, and to convince them that being good fathers was in their best interest, serving to heal the wounds from their own past abuse or neglect. He stressed their part in breaking the cycle and sought to instill the concept that nurturing is a strength, not a weakness. At Christmas he bought gifts for the group members, providing each one with aftershave and a toy truck for the child within. One man cried when he received his truck, commenting that he had never received one as a boy.

One day Lynn had the men make New Year's resolutions for each other, not from a "thou shalt" stance but saying what they would like to see happen with each other. When his turn came to be the focus, one of the men remarked, "You always tell me about spending more time with my kids, but how much time do you spend here?" Lynn, the father of two small boys at the time, reportedly squirmed but recognized the validity of the question. He, too, found the distance between *us* and *them* was not so vast.

In time we added still another group, which we jokingly referred to as the "little t" therapy (headed by a skilled volunteer) as opposed to the "big T" Therapy (run by a degreed professional). Having come a long way from our three-client beginning, we received more referrals than we could handle, but we could not bear the thought of a child possibly being harmed while on a waiting list. What we could offer was afternoon tea or coffee with a sensitive volunteer, Marsha Gordon, who served as hostess. Thanks to her, the parents had a weekly chance to socialize at Cedar House before we found room for them in the "big T" program. With Marilyn as her back-up for crises, Marsha made conversation, put the parents at ease, observed, and later alerted us to the families that needed immediate attention. Thanks to her efforts, we were able to prioritize while offering something besides a waiting list to those who called for help.

Our first group began as an experimental "filial therapy class" and continued as ongoing group therapy. One by one, each succeeding group and class developed in response to a need expressed by those who came for help. Before we knew it, we had a full-blown, comprehensive therapy program, far beyond anything we had envisioned in the beginning. A journey of a thousand miles does indeed begin with the first step.

Chapter 7

Individual Therapy with Parents

Most Cedar House parents attended both group and individual therapy. Dr. Morris Paulson, a psychologist at UCLA who ran a group for abusive parents, once asked why we provided individual therapy in addition to group. We had no quick answer at the time, other than it seemed like the thing to do, but his question led us to explore our rationale.

There were some parents whom we did not include in groups. Occasionally we determined at the intake that the issues with which the family was dealing were too assaultive to the group's sensibilities. We had several cases in which a child had died at the hands of a parent and concern centered on a surviving child. We were convinced of the necessity for parents to face the full details of the traumatic events of abuse, even (perhaps especially) those leading to death, in order to heal. This was handled better in individual sessions. In addition, the parents were already devastated and did not need the risk of a gasp from a shocked group to confirm their self-loathing.

I served as the primary therapist in one case in which a child had died. The mother, Lily, would barely speak for months, responding only with a nod or a soft "no" to my questions and comments. I led her through details of her son's death by guessing how it happened while she nodded or corrected me. Eventually she volunteered details herself, but she was still reserved when she left treatment. I was gratified, but surprised, when she later returned to tell me how much I had helped her, for it seemed to me that I had done most of the talking. She later joined us to speak in public!

We often looked at what could be handled in group and what could not. Some issues were simply too bizarre for the groups. People were not free there to explore the depth of their violent or sexual fantasies, nor did we want them to. Some who tried to do so were diverted to individual sessions for the duration.

In some cases, the parents appeared to be too fragile to handle the give and take of a group. We offered individual therapy to those who appeared to be hanging onto their sanity by a thread, as well as to those who insisted that they could not tolerate sitting in a group. However, one of our goals with them was to bring them into a group when they felt stronger, in order to provide the reparative experience of social support.

If a group member appeared to be stuck, making no progress but voicing the same complaints for weeks, we offered individual sessions to see if we could find out what was creating the emotional log jam. An hour or more focused solely on one individual's situation often revealed the barrier to growth and allowed the therapy to continue more effectively.

When a parent in a group asked for individual sessions, we complied to determine the need. Sometimes new clients had to start with individual therapy because the groups were too full or because their schedules prohibited coming during the group hours.

In both group and individual therapy, our focus stayed on the harm done to the child, how it came to pass, and how to prevent future harm. This meant exploring not only the relationship between the parent and the child but also the dynamics of other relationships within the family and with other important people. While the emphasis on the inner child was not yet in vogue, we had a kind of unformalized inner-child approach. We asked the following questions:

- Can you remember being four (or six or eight)?
- What do you remember?
- Did your family eat together?
- Who sat where?
- Who comforted you when you got hurt?
- Who was there when you were home?
- Did you ever get lost?
- What was that feeling like?
- Has your child ever gotten lost?
- How did you react?
- How did the child react?
- Can you still feel what that child was feeling?

We would lead the talk toward relating the parent's feelings to how the child might feel. Today we would also encourage the adults with sufficiently developed ego strength to try to comfort their own inner child as well as the current child.

It was in individual sessions that we probed for details of the abuse, by asking the following:

- How was the child injured?
- Did you [or he/she] hit with a belt, a fist, an open hand, or some other object?
- Where did the blow land on the child's body?
- How many times did you [or he/she] hit the child?
- What were you feeling at the time?
- What happened just before you [or he/she] struck the child? (Or shook or burned or whatever.)
- How did the child react?
- What did you do afterward?

We did not insist that parents face what they had done all at once but constantly evaluated how much self-disclosure they could tolerate at any given time. We always assessed the parent's state of mind and social supports before ending the session. These were not easy sessions for the clients nor for the therapists.

In both group and individual sessions, we did an ongoing assessment of the level of a parent's anger. Often we asked parents to rate themselves on a scale of one to ten, with ten registering as high rage. Any time they told us a high number, we took them seriously, even if their demeanor belied their self-assessment, for they were telling us that they felt themselves to be in danger of abusing. We could not afford to ignore such a warning. I once advised a therapist whose client had attended one of our "rage meetings" of the woman's self-report of rising rage. The therapist assured me, "She and the children are seen regularly, and they're okay." We learned later that the children were removed soon afterward after being reabused.

We did question the parents' assessments when we saw a discrepancy between their self-reports of no anger and body language that contradicted their words. We had considerable concern for those whose anger remained below the surface, out of reach of rational control. We found that many clients could speak of hurt before they could admit to feeling its companion anger, while others relished expressing their anger while avoiding the acknowledgment of their pain. Believing that anger and pain go hand in hand, we always worked for the clients' awareness of both components of their emotions. We learned that to gain an honest self-assessment required an open, trusting relationship with the client. With the Cedar House population this meant remaining nonjudgmental toward them, for they were highly sensitized to any form of disapproval.

We used individual sessions to take a detailed family history, to provide a concentrated experience of having someone else's full attention, to note clues to disturbed thinking that may not have become apparent in the group, occasionally to teach boundaries of behavior in a gentle fashion, sometimes to model adult coping (for example, making a difficult phone call on their behalf in their presence), and always to validate them: "With what you have experienced, it makes sense that we are here today, having to deal with what has happened."

We did not work with heavy confrontation. We confronted at times but with supportive backup and always stressing that they were not so different from the rest of us who also make mistakes. Given such an approach, it was possible to be honest with them without losing their trust. We could tell a mother that her daughter smelled bad and should be cleaned up for the next week, and she would return the next week with a cleaner child.

Some questioned why we provided such long-term treatment, two years or more for some families. We were interested in the short-term techniques they offered and agreed they could be helpful, but we were skeptical of a magic bullet that would create lasting change sufficient to assure the safety of the children. We saw much of the deficit in parenting skills stemming from a severe deficiency of nurturing in their own backgrounds. Given the emotional "hole in the soul," as author Terry Kellogg has called it, we believed no one could learn to nurture in a day. Yet the child's welfare depended on the parent learning just that. We did believe that many could learn over time with enough reparative experiences.

Chapter 8

The Children

When three-year-old Laura entered the playroom, she ran aimlessly in all directions. Those who tried to engage her found that her speech was unintelligible. When anyone spoke to her, she banged her head against the wall. At snack time she shoved food into her mouth without pause, gorging herself until her mouth could hold no more, then tried to stuff in still more. She had no social skills, little language, and no inner boundaries.

Laura, Sandy's child, was among the first to demonstrate the symptoms that became all too familiar to us in our ongoing work.

In time we learned that Laura had been neglected in her home, sexually abused by neighbors, and physically bruised by her mother's boyfriend, whose handprint on the child's face brought the family to the attention of child protective services. As Laura developed the language and communication skills to tell Pam directly of the episodes of sexual abuse, her mother was emerging from her reclusive lifestyle and becoming more aware of her daughter, providing more protection.

Although eating disorders did not receive the attention then that they have since, we saw the beginnings of them in many children. Urgent overeating was the more common form as children tried to get as much as they could while they could, desperately trying to fill a physical and emotional void. Less common were the children who refused to eat, withholding themselves from receiving anything from the adult in a kind of power struggle.

Anxiety expressed through aimless running or restless movement was not unusual. Some of the children needed to know exactly what was to be found in every corner of the playroom. We found it helped to allay their anxiety when we opened every cupboard door and drawer for them to see, thereby reassuring them that there were no dangers lurking within. If they still could not settle themselves, we tried moving to the back room for a smaller, more manageable space. Most were able to calm down and participate with us and others, once they felt safe enough.*

Often we saw what we called the "plastic smile," the expression in which the mouth smiled but the eyes were sad or anxious. These children, punished when they cried, had learned to smile under stress in a kind of plea: "Don't hurt me." Some children whose abuse was primarily sexual learned not only to smile but to act charming, to be like little adults, to put all of their pain and confusion into an internal compartment, and to present to the world an engaging personality. This fooled many a judge and attorney, who read the behavior to mean that sexual abuse had not occurred or in any case had not hurt the child, unaware of the feelings of phoniness and the vast sense of wrongdoing that haunted these children into adulthood.

A mother who had suffered repeated sexual abuse as a child told of the wonderful training she received for becoming a liar. Her stepfather molested her in the night but acted in daylight as though nothing had happened. From shame and fear, she followed his lead and developed an outward charm, appearing full of life and vitality. However, her internal compartment of pain rose to the surface from time to time. She had tried suicide several times. She found it extremely difficult to give up the plastic smile in adulthood, for this risked exposing her pain.

Ironically, the plastic smile sometimes evoked further punishment. A child who was spanked and then smiled could arouse rage

---

*One exception was a five-year-old boy. The parents, of borderline intelligence, complained of the unruliness of their son, who proved their point with his constant motion and tendency to grab everything in reach. He was beyond the resources of our playroom staff and was ultimately referred to residential care.

The couple returned a short time later with their son and an infant and expressed satisfaction with the change in the boy. He had spent a few days as an inpatient before being sent home on medication. The change was dramatic, for he sat with hands folded, motionless, eyes dulled. The parents were so pleased with the change that they used the medication to quiet the baby when he cried! After our warning to the parents of the dangers of medicating without a doctor's orders, we notified the residential program's doctor, noting the importance of evaluating parents' capabilities before counting on medication to solve a child's problem. Unfortunately we did not see the family again.

in the punishing parent, who read this as defiance or indifference. Even for the child spared punishment, the smile could prove counterproductive. Some assumed that when a child smiled, there was no real problem. Others detected the smile as false, but called it "manipulative," missing the point that the manipulation was to prevent a previously experienced pain. The onus remained on the child. When these children could show their sadness openly, they were on their way to healing.

Some children retreated to an inner world when under stress. A few reportedly began doing this when they were being abused to escape the assault, if only in their minds. They described their inner retreats, some as isolated as an unpopulated moon, others alive with foes to vanquish, still others under the care of a benevolent God. (This last may seem benign, but when a child we had treated in the past later attempted suicide to get to that better world, we recognized the danger of too much preoccupation with God's realm amid insufficient earthly comfort.) Many times these children appeared dull or disconnected in relation to adults. Dull they were not, for they were often quite busy in their inner worlds. They were disconnected to our world, which was our cue to explore the possibility of an inner world.*

A five-year-old girl comes to mind. We had a difficult time getting a handle on this child. One day she made an offhand remark about something "on the moon." I asked, "Have you ever been on the moon?" Surprised, she admitted that she went there a lot. I asked if I could come along. She agreed, and from then on, we established a connection. Until then we had occupied two different, unrelated worlds.

A ten-year-old girl, Stacy, made little eye contact and seemed out in space herself—until her group discussed their sexual experiences. Suddenly, dramatically, she emerged from her world and joined us, sharing that she had been molested by her father. All of

---

*I broached the question of an inner world by asking, "When you don't want to be someplace, do you go somewhere else in your mind?" I was amused when a colleague who consulted me on a case later told of asking the child, "Do you sometimes go out of your mind?" His question worked, however, for he learned of the child's inner world.

her energies had gone into trying to cope internally with the trauma, leaving no energy for socializing.

We observed that many of the sexually abused children were overachievers in school while others, like Stacy, were almost non-functional in school. Like their parents, their responses to the abuse tended to the extremes.

Some of the children liked to play dead. We read this as the child's implied question: Do I exist? Do I matter? When a child went inert, we made a great fuss about the importance of saving this child who was so special. They loved the attention, of course, and often wanted to play dead again and again, week after week. We treated the young-sters who repeatedly played dead as potential future suicide candidates. On occasion we were challenged as to whether we weren't reinforcing the behavior with so much attention, but, given what we were hearing from their parents about feelings of emptiness and nonexistence, we did not want to leave the children feeling the same. In any case, the behavior extinguished itself on its own when the children got their fill. Many of the "victims" later joined us in becoming rescuers.

Many sexually abused children presented a facade of pseudo-maturity, acting like premature and unconsciously seductive adults. A four-year-old boy, startled when a girl entered the room, greeted her provocatively, "Hello, baby!" Very young girls came to Cedar House wearing lipstick and jewelry. They danced like teeny-boppers and sang in sexy tones. One seven-year-old girl, meeting me for the first time, sang in a remarkably precocious voice, "I am not a little girl any more," her hips swaying. As she saw it, she could no longer be a little girl after having sex with her stepfather.

Many children who have been battered or sexually assaulted tend to associate any kind of touching with abuse. While sitting restlessly on my lap, four-year-old Laura fell backward, accidentally hit her head, and indignantly accused me of hitting her. Among those who have been sexually abused, some false allegations may arise out of the tendency to associate touch anywhere on the body with past sexual stimulation.

A graduate student of psychology at California State University of Long Beach, Helen Johnson, studied the behavior of abused children at Cedar House, comparing them with a control group of nonabused children. To her surprise, on two different behavior scales she found more passive behavior among Cedar House children than in the control group. To us this made sense, for an abused child's survival might well depend on compliance. We speculated that only in later years, as the child became bigger and more powerful, would it be safe enough for the rage from former abuse to erupt.

I recently learned the unfortunate outcome of one of our early cases. A private investigator, working for the county counsel's office in another state, appeared in Long Beach, seeking mitigating circumstances for a young man convicted of murder and facing the death penalty. A fire had wiped out Cedar House's records of the family, but I vividly recalled the mother. The child had experienced a kidnapping, severe physical abuse, and a series of foster homes as he grew up. As a small boy, he did not act up in our playroom, but he did grow up to kill his wife.

Years after the study at Cedar House, another graduate student did a study of the sexually abused young children at our next program, Sarah Center. She did not find as much approach/reject behavior as she expected, but what she found was a higher level of aggression among the sexually abused children than in the control group. This interested us in view of our finding that the parents of physically abused children had so often been sexually abused as children.

We concluded, without surprise, that abuse in any form leaves residues of anger and feelings of aggression. The two studies would indicate that those who perceived themselves to be in physical danger for their lives from battering or abandonment were more likely to develop the survival defense of passivity, trying to keep life-threatening episodes at bay. Those who were sexually mistreated but not battered were more likely to express their aggression openly. Almost all of them, however, acted out when convinced it was safe to do so. Pam saw aggressive behavior in the physically abused children who trusted her, but the children were more compliant in the presence of the researcher, showing more caution than the Sarah Center children in a similar situation. In any case, the aggressive feelings of both physically and sexually abused children, left unaddressed, tend to stay with them into adulthood, sometimes with tragic consequences.

Chapter 9

Group Therapy with Children

The children's groups were more structured than the adult groups, but we still emphasized responding to issues that the children raised, rather than insisting on an agenda. They were free to choose their own activities for the first half hour while the treatment team engaged with them and took their emotional temperature of the day. Was any of their behavior unusual? Who was acting out today? Was anyone especially anxious or angry, happy or sad?

This was followed by an hour of structured activities, starting with a "circle time" in which the children brought chairs and had a chance to tell what was going on in their lives. The treatment team then introduced other activities such as crafts, music, art, stories, or books related to feelings. This was followed by more free time, a five-minute snack with positive feedback to the children on what the team had observed that day, and clean-up. The group ended with a five-minute story, a song, or a happy thought. Though the children may have dealt with some heavy issues in the course of the morning, it was important to send them home in as peaceful a mood as possible, to minimize any chance of behavior that might elicit abuse.

The willingness to sit in the circle and take part in the discussion was a giant step forward for many who had experienced little structure in their lives. Of course, it took time, consistency of staff and volunteers, clarity in what we expected of them, and sometimes maturation for them to become comfortable participants in the circle. We stressed the importance of the volunteers' long-term commitment to the children's groups to give the youngsters a sense of stability and security. We usually had two or three volunteers in each group.

Because the groups were formed mostly by deciding which parents belonged with whom, Pam did not have the luxury of choosing which children to include. (Larry Hanna, our volunteer psychologist, often remarked that Pam had the hardest job of all.) The morning groups served preschoolers, who ranged in age from infants to five-year-olds. Volunteers who enjoyed holding babies took the infants in hand. We did not expect miracles from the toddlers, but it was always a milestone when a two-year-old lugged a chair to join the group discussion. Each child was assured that he or she was an important part of the circle. The restless ones found reassuring laps, but we put out a chair for each to signal their inclusion as separate individuals in the group whenever they were ready.

In the evening couples' group and parenting class, and in the summer, we became acquainted with the school-age children. The structure of the children's groups remained the same.

As the children interacted with each other, we took the opportunity to teach some skills for conflict resolution. "Instead of hitting Johnny and grabbing his toy, try offering another toy to trade." We focused on what they felt and made an effort to help them hear what the other person felt. Sometimes, rather than suggesting a solution, I reflected their words to each other, insisting that they figure out how to deal with the situation without hitting.

> "He took my toy and I had it first!"
> "Johnny says you took his toy away while he was playing with it."
> "I wanted to play with it."
> "Jimmy says he wants to play with it, too."
> "I had it first!"
> "Johnny says he had it first."
> "Okay, here!"

The exchanges did not always end so quickly, of course, but I found that with patience, occasionally with assurance to them that they could figure out what to do, they eventually did find a way out to the satisfaction of both. I was often reminded of a quote from Lord Chesterton: "Many a man would rather you heard his story than granted his request."

Following a visit to the Therapeutic Nursery at the Department of Mental Health, where we observed a confrontive approach with preschool children that encouraged—nay, insisted on—the verbalizing of their fears and their feelings, Pam sought in her gentler manner to encourage the very young children to use words more often to express themselves. From time to time, she was deeply moved as they did exactly that. In a group of seven girls, ages five to seven, she encouraged a conversation by asking if any of them had ever felt angry. One girl responded by telling of the sexual abuse she had suffered. Other group members chimed in with descriptions of their experiences of abuse, commenting on how mad it had made them and how much it had hurt. Pam did not need to ask leading questions but simply listened with her usual empathy, noting that once the children felt safe, they were remarkably open with their stories and their feelings. She reminisced recently, "I thought to myself, 'This is great, they're saying it,' but at the same time, within myself, I had to deal with what was coming out of the mouths of all those beautiful little faces!"

During the first ten minutes of group, Pam or one of the volunteers sat with the adults to hear of the children's behavior or problems in the family during the preceding week. This helped both for gathering information needed for the therapy and to focus the parents' attention on their children. Later, in the last fifteen minutes of group, a team member came to the adult group to provide feedback on the children's behavior that day. Sometimes we asked the children what we should tell the parents to encourage their reflecting on what had happened of importance to them. Now and then Pam had a question for the adults. Little Carla wanted to pull everyone's hair today. Was anything going on that the staff needed to know? Well, yes, Carla's mother admitted she had pulled the child's hair that morning. The parents could not help but notice the connection between their own behavior and that of the child when faced with such stark examples.

Other times, however, the one giving feedback simply described some of the antics that had impressed or amused the team. The fondness for the children that the team members demonstrated was not lost on the parents. For instance, though conscientious with the job of raising her three small sons, Sophie took little pleasure in the baby, Timothy, the child who was "one too many." Richard O'Leary, a volunteer, developed a bond with little Timothy, who was of an unusually sunny disposition. Over time, as Richard lit up each time the baby arrived, Sophie began to see Timothy through Richard's eyes, as a delight rather than a chore.

Pam wrote a guide for the new staff and volunteers who helped with the treatment of the children in the playroom. In it she stressed the importance of the team's communication with each other, for we did not expect those dealing with hurt children to be unaffected by what they heard and saw. The way to a strong treatment team was mutual support, lending our strength of the moment to anyone struggling with intense personal reactions to a child's story. "When you're hurting, sometimes you may see things in kids that you feel you can't handle, like fighting or screaming," Pam wrote. "Tell someone. We are a team, and that's what it's all about—to be there for each other. Groups are very exciting, heavy, fun, sad, rewarding, painful, and important."

Along with delight and amusement, of course, came the rest of the range of feelings. Staff members became aware of their wells of sadness that developed as children described what was done to them. In the playroom we sometimes had volunteers and occasionally staff members (for we are not immune) who experienced painfully empathetic responses to a child's story or behavior, usually when it triggered something from their own backgrounds. Some cried, some withdrew and became inaccessible, and others rallied and carried on but broke down later. Pam's advice to share with the team could not be overemphasized. We did not want our team members feeling as helpless as the children.

Even Pam, who gave unstintingly of herself for four years, decided to leave Cedar House in 1979, feeling the need to be among "sparkly-eyed children" for a while.

Chapter 10

Individual Therapy with Children

We offered individual play therapy to children for a variety of reasons. We responded to the need for individual attention in times of crisis: family break-up, violence in the home, eviction or any other uprooting move, or, in two cases, a child returned after being kidnapped. If we sensed that a parent was too distressed or preoccupied to give attention to the child, we offered individual sessions to both for the duration. If a child asked for a play session, we provided it, figuring that the child must have something to tell us.

Some received individual therapy when we determined that their disclosures could be too disturbing to the group. When a five-year-old girl told in group of her mother sexually abusing her (news to us at the time), the shock of the other children was clear. "Your *mother?!*" We saw this child and her mother individually to learn the details and to provide a safer setting for them (and perhaps for us) to deal with the disclosure.

Some children received individual therapy because their parents were unable or unwilling to attend a group, or because the staff determined that group would not be the appropriate forum for the work required of the parent. When we dealt with a family in which a child had died from abuse, we began with individual therapy for the parent and for the surviving child(ren).

In the play sessions, we followed guidelines formulated by Virginia Axline, Haim Ginott, and Clark Moustakas, with some modifications. We provided projective materials (e.g., crayons and paper, paint, playdough, dolls and a dollhouse, animal figures, puppets, toy telephones, doctor kits, etc.). The child was given the lead in how to make use of the toys. While we set firm limits against harm to persons or property, we accepted the child's expression of feelings in other modes.

If a child wanted to do something unacceptable, we offered another avenue of expression for the feeling involved. For instance, a four-year-old girl who was angry with me showed a determination to twist my nose. I drew a simple face outline that I called "Bobbi" and suggested she could twist that instead. She crumpled it and stomped on it, threw it away, and returned to my nose. I drew another and another in self-defense until the floor was ankle high in paper, commenting only that I could see she was *really angry* today. When the urgency of the action finally passed, she was able to say that she was angry because I had not been there the previous week when she came. I assured her that I knew she missed me, that I did not go away because of anything she did, and that I would be there from now on unless I was sick or on vacation.

Sometimes we simply reflected what the child said or did as a signal of our acceptance and to assure that we heard what the child was telling us. A child absorbed in setting up figures in a dollhouse might say, "She goes in here," and we might respond, "Oh, she goes there." (I once heard a teacher remark, "I got a college degree to learn how to say 'Oh.'") Usually the child would continue in his or her train of thought, but occasionally one would ask, "Why do you say what I say?" At that point we simply observed or joined in the play at the child's direction.

When children expressed an urge to take a playroom toy home, we called on their imaginations. While we were clear that the toys stayed in Cedar House, we tried to give it to them in playful fantasy: "Wouldn't that be fun to have it with you every day? What would you do with it?" We found the children readier to relinquish the object when they could at least play with the idea. We suggested this approach for parents as they shopped with demanding children in a store, rather than giving in resentfully to a child's demands or becoming angry that the child even asked.

We provided words to describe the feelings that the children demonstrated, for some had not yet learned this vocabulary. I asked Candy, a four-year-old girl who lived an isolated life with her mother, what made her sad. She replied, "Disneyland." As I explored her answer, I discovered that she was confused by the words "sad" or "mad." Words of feeling were not spoken in her home and, I learned, were words that the mother found threatening. Before Candy could comfortably figure out and express what she felt, her mother also needed to become familiar herself with the nuances and acceptability of feelings.

We made frequent use of the words "happy," "sad," "angry," "mad," "scary," "frightening," "lonely," "disappointed," and others. I have created "feeling books" with children, listing what makes them happy, angry, sad, and scared (one feeling per page), then enlisting their help in adding other feelings. Often the children liked having their responses read back to them in later sessions, reminding them of how they felt in the past, on good days and bad. I have gained a great deal of information and been taken by surprise by some of the entries in these books.

Almost all of the abused children reported nightmares full of monsters, witches, werewolves, and the like. We worked to empower them to face their fears by overcoming their own monsters. We asked the children to describe and then draw the monsters, externalizing them, and then decide what to do with them. Tear them up? Tack them firmly on the bulletin board? In any case, the drawings stayed at Cedar House so the monster could not go home with them.

We noted that preschool children who were told that monsters were not real remained unconvinced.* We assured them, however, that the one thing that will drive monsters away faster than anything is to talk about them. "They want to be secret," we would tell them. "If you see a monster and you go tell someone about it and then you try to show it to them, it won't be there." We explained our thinking to the parents, both to avert the chance that they might shame the child for being silly and to alert them that they might be awakened in the night if the child dreamed of a monster. When we came across a parent who objected to being awakened, we role-played with the child to chase a phantom monster, yelling "Go away!" Convincing them they could do this even in their dreams, we rehearsed what the children would do in a future nightmare. We also suggested flashlights, for it was of course known that monsters do not like the light.

---

*A professional friend told of his adult children reminiscing about their childhood monster that lurked under a stairway. He commented that he had not known a monster lived there. They replied, "We knew if we told you, you would say it wasn't real."

Now and then a child or a parent devised another solution, once they caught on to the principle of empowerment. One mother gave her four-year-old boy a spray bottle to squirt the monster. In all seriousness he informed us, "The lemon spray works much better than the cinnamon spray!"

Most children's nightmares ceased as they found they did not have to feel helpless in the presence of the scary beings of their imaginations. If a child's nightmares persisted, we looked for the cause in the real world.

The Disney book *The Rescuers* resonated deeply with some of the especially frightened children we met. Most preschoolers did not have the attention span for an entire reading of the book. A few, however, became engrossed and asked for it to be read again on the spot. We noticed that these were children living in homes with frequent outbursts of violence. These were children who longed for rescue.

Part of our work with abused children, those who were pseudo-mature, consisted of giving them permission to be children. This often led to considerable regression. Having become too quickly adult in manner, they needed to fill in the earlier gap. Some wanted to be rocked and otherwise treated like babies. We obliged, trusting that they would eventually get their fill. If an eight-year-old asked to suck on a bottle, we allowed it while reassuring the mother that this behavior was limited to the playroom and that this, too, would pass. Some took longer than others, but none stayed with the bottle forever.

We talked with some of the children about the advantages of being little: "I couldn't crawl under the crib because I'm too big, but I'll bet that's something you can do." Invariably they demonstrated their newly valued ability, relieving them of the pressure of having to act older than their age.

We encouraged use of the child's imagination. "If you had a magic key," Pam would ask, "what would it open?" A "magic wand," the key to desires, served to elicit the child's wishes. With toy telephones a child was invited to help another child with a problem, first defining what that problem might be. Pam used imagery along with drawing, having them imagine animals, for instance, and then draw them, or find a way to draw their anger and their fears. The monster drawings served the same purpose.

I sometimes used imagery for relaxation, transporting children to a safe place in their minds. First, I explored a time and place where they felt safe, this becoming the setting for the imagery. For the few children who could not recall a time when they were safe, I lent them my safe place, giving them permission to use it until they found their own safe spot.

Sometimes I did drawings for the young children to learn who was most on their minds and, in some cases, to provide them an outlet for their feelings. I made an outline of a person, then asked, "Should this be a man or a woman? Happy or mad or sad? Curly or straight hair? Long or short? What color? What would you like to do with him [her] now? What do you think should happen to him [her]?" Those who had been abused often described the offenders and thought up all kinds of horrible fates for them (put them in jail, stab them with a knife, tear them up, throw them in the trash, etc.). Some showed mixed feelings, kissing them before putting them in jail. In some cases of sexual abuse, we gained useful information regarding the identity of the perpetrators while the children had an opportunity to vent their feelings, usually anger, on the drawings. I was always careful to follow the child's lead in this activity without prying for information. If the child wanted to describe a mother, kiss her and let it go at that, that is what the child got to do.

Always, always, we assumed that the children would tell us their stories, in play and in words, if we paid attention long enough. Sometimes the stories took a long time to tell. For a year, Ashley, age four, stuck to her tale of being molested by a teacher, but her bizarre behavior continued to puzzle us. When her father moved out, she finally revealed that the offender was her father, not the teacher. At this point her behavior improved dramatically. We learned then that her fear, a reflection of her mother's concern, had been that if she offended her father, he would abandon the family and they would have no food to eat.

Could we have gotten the story earlier by doing a better job of prying? In her case, I doubt it. She was not ready to divulge the secret until her mother was ready to hear it. From Ashley, we learned how long a very young child can sustain a secret, even making up details when asked, to protect a family.

Chapter 11

Sexual Abuse

The Cedar House staff entered the field of sexual abuse reluctantly, but the children gave us no choice. Tommy, age three, could not be ignored as he assaulted the volunteers in the playroom, trying to rub their breasts while breathing hard.

In her first session, seven-year-old Kim sang in a sexy tone, "I'm not a little girl any more," with body language to match. She described how her stepfather fondled her and asked her to masturbate him. In time Kim disclosed, first to Jane Gold of the Therapeutic Nursery and then to me, that the mother she lived with was not her real mother. In her mind, her real mother was a black cat in the zoo, kept in a cage and unable to come for her.

We were not ready for this. In 1975 we naively assumed we would simply work on stopping parents from battering their children. Sexual abuse was still in the closet, even among most professionals. We had no idea what to do with tiny sex offenders, but we knew we had to do something.

Seeking someone with more experience with the problem, we found a child psychologist who agreed to consult with us. When we described Tommy's behavior, however, he remarked that he had not treated a child that young. We presented our tentative plan of action: to deal with the child in the same way we treated other children, allowing him to play out his conflicts (on dolls, not people) while we provided appropriate limits. Did he think this would help the child in the long run? We will never forget his reply: "It is doubtful. You can find out in twenty years." He had no better plan to offer.

We heard of Dr. Roland Summit, a psychiatrist with a reputation as an expert on child sexual abuse. I attended a workshop in which he served as a panel member, but he talked of fathers and surrogate fathers who molested their adolescent daughters. I later asked him what to do with a three-year-old boy who showed all the signs of sexual experience. Like the psychologist, he had not dealt with such a situation. Shortly thereafter, however, he agreed to consult with us.

Dr. Summit, who quickly became Roland to us, recently reminisced about one of his first meetings at Cedar House. As we talked, he noted our disappointment that he did not have more definitive answers to our questions on how to proceed in this highly charged area. We had indeed hoped to avoid reinventing the wheel, but in the absence of an established wheel, we accepted his offer to help us explore the problems.

We were aware that Roland had to defend his views among skeptical colleagues in the psychiatric community of the day when he accepted the premise that sexual abuse could be real, not inevitably fantasized. The strain of being a lone voice in a sea of doubt must have showed that day, for Marilyn offered him a blanket. As Roland described it, "Here was I, the professional who could be expected to maintain some vestige of dignity, sitting under a blanket and loving the experience of being triple-mothered!"

Roland met with us monthly, sharing his observations as he consulted with professionals throughout the United States and abroad. Often he articulated our findings while we struggled for words to express them. He saw us through good times and bad, and he remains a close friend to this day.

We finally took a deep collective breath and purchased two anatomically correct baby dolls, knowing we would see more than we wanted to see. Since we had few guidelines to go by at the time, our work was experimental. We acquired the dolls in the belief that the children needed tools to express their traumas. We saw children reenact beatings and hair-pulling. If they were traumatized by a sex act, we figured they needed to reenact that, too. Better on the dolls than on our volunteers.

When four-year-old Laura first saw the dolls, she undressed the boy doll, covered her face and said, "Oh, he has a ponytail." Uncovering her face, she said, "You want me to suck you," and added to Pam, "He wants you to suck him. I will show you how," and proceeded to do so. She told of doing this a lot at "Ben's house," adding, "Pete wants to kiss my pussy. Pete puts his ponytail in my pussy like this," demonstrating the act with a thrusting motion. Laura then threw the doll across the room, saying angrily, "I don't want to suck your ponytail! Leave me alone! Leave me alone!"

In his sessions Tommy performed the sex act in detail with the girl doll. Other children were equally graphic.

We explored with Sandy, Laura's mother, what could account for her child's behavior. Ben and Pete, we learned, were neighbors, men who had invited Laura into their home during the day. Until then Sandy had been pleased that these nice men were kind to her daughter and that she had some respite from looking after a restless child. She cared about Laura, but she was too preoccupied to be sensitive to the danger to her daughter. Following the disclosure, Laura was kept home.

As for Kim, whose mother was supposed to be a cat, her stepfather moved out of their home and was not permitted to see her again, except for one session with Jane Gold and me. In this session he apologized to Kim, assuring her that what he had done with her was wrong and that it was not her fault but his. She listened closely, looking distressed. Thereafter we worked to help her to be a little girl again.

In time at Cedar House, in our later work at Sarah Center (which initially served only young sexually abused children and their families), and in our private practice, we have become far more familiar with the needs of sexually abused children.

These children had experienced a total loss of control over what was done to their bodies. A sexually exploited three-year-old once told me plaintively, "I couldn't get *out!*" When they were bossy, trying to take total control in the playroom, we honored the need even as we set some broad guidelines. If a child told us, "Go over there!" we kept our distance until we saw the child becoming more comfortable. If the child told us to leave the room, we did not, but we gave reassurance that we would stay "way over here" to give them a sense of safety.

As for the reenactment of the sexual abuse, we found that it did help the children to express what had occurred, as well as helping us to gain information for purposes of court hearings.

Too often the legal needs of the case came into conflict with the therapeutic needs of the child. Prosecutors were concerned that the children's testimony not be contaminated by their inclusion in a group, but we found group therapy to be the most beneficial form of treatment for reducing a child's feeling of being the only one with this shameful problem. This left us with the choice of either withholding, often for months, their chance to share with peers and feel themselves a part of the human race or jeopardizing the court proceedings.

When we suspect sexual abuse, we try to get as much information as possible without leading questions. Over the years we have developed the following approach for interviewing young children:

In our first meeting we determine whether the children know why they have come and, if not, we explain that Cedar House is a place to talk about anything that bothers them. We start with non-threatening questions. With preschool children we bring out crayons to determine if they know their colors, for if they later tell of something coming out of a man's penis, we will ask what color it was. We also provide paper for drawing, to provide an outlet for any anxiety they may be feeling. We find out how high they can count and determine if they can use numbers to count objects. Using a doll (not anatomical), we go over their names for the various body parts. Sometimes merely naming the vagina or penis (the former known by many colorful appellations such as "the flower," "the self,"* "the pussy," or "the peepee") elicits disclosure of being inappropriately touched in that area.

We explore family relationships. We make figures out of clay and name them for family members or, if the parent has named a perpetrator, we might give the figure that name. If the child pounds the figure flat, we invite comment with a remark such as, "Wow, that took care of him! I wonder what he did to deserve that!"

We ask about things that bother them, things that have hurt them, or that felt bad. "What makes you mad? What makes you sad? What scares you? Has anyone ever done something you didn't like?" We might give a series of examples: "Did you ever have a spanking? Has anyone called you names? Did anyone ever accuse you of

---

*This name for the vaginal area bothered me. Any time this girl used the term "myself," she was identified by her sex organ. Unfortunately I was unable to persuade her mother to use another term.

doing something you didn't do? Has anyone ever t
private parts?" (It is one question in a list.)

At some point we might bring forth a coloring book on go..
touch and bad touch. Sometimes the drawing of a man's hand in the
back of a girl's underpants elicits comments such as, "That happened to me." The picture of a girl sitting on a grandfatherly lap
occasionally arouses discomfort and a remark such as, "She doesn't
like that." We then explore the child's individual experience on
laps. If the child does not volunteer any more comments, we finish
the book by role-playing what to do if someone invites him or her to
get in a strange car. By then, needing an outlet for physical energy,
they love running across the room and "telling."

Once a child speaks of a possible sexual experience, however, we
ask specific questions.

- What happened?
- Who did it?
- Where were you?
- How did it start?
- Did they say anything?
- How did they do it?
- Can you show me with the dolls?
- Did you have your clothes on?
- Did they have their clothes on?
- How did it feel? If the child describes seeing a man's penis, we
  ask if it was up or down.
- If they describe "rain" from a man's "peepee," we ask what
  color it was.
- Was anyone else there?
- Who was there?
- What did you do?
- Did anyone say anything?
- What did they say?
- What did you say?
- How did it end?
- Did this ever happen again?

To the last question, one girl replied sadly, "Every day."

Sometimes, after the child has told the story, we test for suggestibility. If they have placed the dolls in a particular position, later in the session we might place the dolls in a different position and ask, "Is that the way it was?" Usually they correct us, returning the dolls to the former position and thereby strengthening their credibility.

After we have as much information as we believe is forthcoming, our final question retreats from fact-finding to therapy: "What do you think should happen to this person [the perpetrator]?" Most of the offenders, represented in drawings or a doll, are given some kind of unhappy fate, whether a spanking, incarceration behind a piece of furniture, a stabbing with a pencil, a thorough stomping, being thrown in the trash, or other imaginative punishments.

Sometimes disclosures come in drawings, in play with figures in a dollhouse, or in casual conversation. Children usually feel freer to talk when engaged in an activity with their hands, such as drawing or molding clay. Group therapy is helpful at all ages, for children often share information more freely among peers, but there is the drawback, as noted, of diminishing credibility in court proceedings.

We finally acquired the expensive anatomical family dolls. Their use has since become controversial, seen as leading or titillating the children. I believe the dolls are helpful—Laura's response to the sight of the "ponytail" led to quicker protection for her than might have taken place otherwise—but the work can go on with or without these visual aids. When we began, four-year-old Rachel used two dolls, differentiated only by their clothes, to lay the boy doll on top of the girl doll and then moved the boy in an unmistakable rhythmic thrusting motion. She did not need the overt sexual organs to demonstrate the act.

Some children, of course, are reluctant to speak of their sexual experiences, particularly those who have been threatened or told not to tell. Sometimes their nightmares are clues to what has occurred. In one case, in which the offender had threatened to kill the child's cat if she told, she did not name the perpetrator until the cat died.

I have insisted on three sessions to evaluate whether a child has in fact been molested, unless the facts are too stark to deny. Too often the situation is murky. I want to test the consistency of the child's story and have as clear a picture as possible. Many children, like adults, need time to become comfortable enough to share details of

an experience that caused them shame. In a few cases we pro
child abuse reports by waiting. A boy who had described a
experience as though it were his own later told us in which movie he
had seen the act on cable TV. We recommended that the parents
supervise his television viewing, but we did not make a report.

While treating young children who had been sexually abused, I
puzzled over how to help them trust their experience over the denial
of parents. Young children believe what their parents tell them,
which can leave some terribly confused. A four-year-old told of her
father putting his finger in her vagina. At a later session she told me
he had not. I asked if she remembered telling me he did. Yes, she
did. Did she believe it then? Yes. What changed her mind? "My
daddy told me he didn't do it."

Another four-year-old, Cindy, told of digital penetration by her
father and of witnessing him throwing her mother down, hurting
her. The mother corroborated the story of violence, but the father
adamantly denied that he had ever done this. The court found insufficient evidence of sexual abuse and awarded unmonitored visits.
The child refused to speak of molestation any further but played
week after week that she and I were in a trap.

> One day I hit the table suddenly. Cindy jumped and asked,
> "Why did you do that?"
> "What?"
> "You hit the table!"
> "No, I didn't."
> "You did, too, hit the table!" She yelled, shaking an enraged
> finger in my face.
> "What makes you think I hit the table?"
> "I saw you!"
> "Did you hear anything?"
> "Yeah."
> "Did you feel the table shake?"
> "Yeah. It shaked."
> "Good for you! You know it happened even if I say it
> didn't."

This became Cindy's favorite game. She would come into the
playroom, turn her head, say, "Hit the table!" and replay the scene.

Her father eventually admitted in the child's presence that he had been violent with the mother, although still denying the molestation. Cindy began to allow us to escape the traps.

We never learned exactly how Tommy, the one who catapulted us into the sex abuse field, came to be sexually traumatized, but we were aware of the sexualized atmosphere in his home. His parents admitted to having sexual orgies that he probably witnessed. His father masturbated in front of the family, explaining to us that he was a "seven-days-a-week man married to a once-a-week woman." The walls of the home displayed sexual pictures until we recommended their removal to reduce the stimulation to the boy. Tommy's mother had been molested as a child and tended to interpret any touch as sexual. Since both parents were obsessed with sex and unfamiliar with what was appropriate for a child, Tommy had plenty of opportunity for sexual stimulation. It is possible he was himself molested, though we never established that as a fact. In any case, his preoccupation with sex diminished as his and the family's treatment progressed.

Now and then Tommy's sexualized behavior resurfaced, and we again had to explore what was going on. Generally we found an incident or circumstance—an X-rated movie or the like—that accounted for the resurgence of his sexual preoccupation. On one occasion Tommy himself alerted Pam to a problem, saying as he came in the door, hand to his head, "Pam, I need a play session!"

Tommy's family stayed with us for more than two years. His mother called us now and then for years afterward, sometimes to seek advice, sometimes just to make contact. The last we heard, Tommy was a teenager, occasionally in trouble for fighting but doing well in school. He sometimes asked to go for counseling. We believe that our work with him as a preschooler provided a safety valve in his future, for he had learned early, when his stress became too heavy, to say, "I need a play session!"

To our knowledge, his mother's fear of Tommy becoming a sex offender have turned out to be unfounded.

Chapter 12

Other Approaches

Since we focused on child abuse, a problem of behavior that was to be found in a wide range of clientele, there was no possibility of finding a one-size-fits-all approach.

We started our first group as a "filial therapy class," teaching parents to do play therapy with their own children. Because we planned to serve low-income clients among others, we chose to provide sets of toys for each parent in the class. The sets included crayons and paper, small family figures, a few animal figures, handmade puppets, toy telephones, a doctor kit, a punch clown, and a recipe for homemade craft dough for the parents to make. They were instructed to spend thirty minutes each week, alone and hopefully uninterrupted, with one child (age ten or under) and the toys, which were to be available only during the play sessions for the duration of the twelve-week class. The mothers were to allow the child to choose which toys to use, follow the child's lead without directing the play (easier said than done!), and accept any statements or actions, stopping only those actions that could harm others or property. Then they were to report at our next meeting what the child had done and said during the session.

Typically the mothers reported that not much happened, but as they gave details, it became clear that the child had expressed a great deal. The play sessions called for the parent to focus on the child in a different way from the usual, often bringing their habitual responses into awareness. Even to describe what the child did, the parent had to pay attention.

By using this approach, we hoped to give the parents a sense of helping their own children. Some did indeed express pride in working with their children, and most began to see the children in a different light. We cannot claim a high level of success in maternal insights, however, since many of our clients dealt with the world at a very concrete level. Some mothers were uncomfortable with having to focus on the child that long. One parent termed it "intolerable," a poignant measure of her discomfort with mothering. But there were incidents worth noting.

Ruth's four-year-old son Kevin, recently returned from foster placement, chose a dollhouse (which Ruth provided) and family figures for his play. He placed several family members in the house, including Ruth's incarcerated boyfriend, then picked up the figure representing himself and asked, "Where does he go?" Sensitive enough to hear the unspoken question "Where do I belong?", Ruth reassured him that he belonged in the house with her. Until this play session she had viewed Kevin as a happy-go-lucky four-year-old, free of anxiety.

Pam observed that Laura's speech was not that of a normal three-year-old. Knowing Sandy, her mother, we could believe that Laura had little opportunity to use language at home.

In a play session with Sandy, Laura dialed a toy telephone to various people who, she said, were "not home." She then threw the telephone in a fit of anger. We interpreted to Sandy that her daughter was saying in effect, "No one talks to me, and it makes me mad." We arranged for someone from Cedar House to call Laura periodically. Sandy not only accepted the arrangement but reminded us of it as she left. We also encouraged Sandy to talk more with her daughter, hoping this would serve to make her more aware of the child's daily presence. In a matter of weeks, Laura's speech began to improve.

We did not continue with filial therapy after the twelve weeks, although we later offered it in another mothers' group and in a separate class led by Arthur Kraft and me. Generally we found the approach to be more effective among our higher functioning parents. While many of the children (not all) enjoyed and looked forward to the play sessions with their mothers, it took effort on our part to get the parents to do the play sessions consistently, for that required a self-discipline that many had not developed. Moreover, we found that children who would promptly reenact their episodes of abuse in the playroom would not touch the subject directly with the parents who hurt them. While some mothers expressed feeling closer to the child, the child still did not feel safe enough in the relationship to say, "You hurt me!" For this the child needed an outside ally.

Role-playing proved effective for working on relationships, communication skills, and conflict resolution. We also used role-playing to prepare group members for a new experience that might be difficult for them such as approaching a prospective employer or appearing in court.

Marilyn and Clara were especially skilled at role-playing. They would suddenly engage in a mock verbal battle or respond with helplessness or sarcasm, whatever was appropriate to the context. If a group member complained that her mother criticized her housekeeping, Clara might turn to Marilyn and say, "Do you really like living in a pigsty? When will you ever learn to keep house?" Marilyn responded with a whine or defiance, depending on the style of the complainer. Often the two of them moved into the role-playing so smoothly, without warning, that they startled the group members, but they invariably captured their attention. We then focused on the participants' reactions and what in the interaction had affected them. Some confessed that they expected Clara and Marilyn to come to blows. We explored what could be changed to elicit less tension while dealing with the problem. The scene would be replayed as group members proposed different approaches and took various roles.

In one individual session, a father, Frank, described a harsh scolding he had delivered to his young son. Marilyn, all five feet two inches of her, stood on a table to deliver a similar scolding to him, demonstrating how it must have been for the boy. When she resumed her caring manner, Frank reported that she had truly scared him to the point that his hands were sweating. He made the empathetic leap to what his son must have felt.

Frank's wife recently contacted us after many years to thank us for Cedar House's help. She gave the program credit for teaching Frank how to be a father and for the fact that the family was still intact. When asked what her most memorable moment at Cedar House had been, she replied, "In group when Marilyn made Frank sit on the floor and she stood on the coffee table and yelled at him.

That was when the change in Frank came about. He finally understood what it felt like."

Like others, we found *drawing* very useful. One exercise proved especially evocative of early emotions. As we explored their backgrounds, we often asked people to draw their households at mealtimes. Some could not recall a single time of sitting with their parents at meals; some told of eating in front of the television with family members but without communication; others described who sat where at the dinner table, commenting on who sat beside mom (her favorite, or the littlest, or the one who gave the most trouble) or dad (his favorite or the one he enjoyed harassing), who sat directly opposite (looking across the table with affection or hostility or with the secretly shared reactions of siblings in difficult circumstances).

As we gave a talk in a high school class, Clara brought up the question of who sat where at the dinner table. We should have known by then, but we were struck by the intensity of the feelings that this aroused among the students. More than one wept as they told of eating alone because their parents were not home or were involved with the television.

We tried *sculpturing* with nine-year-old Katie, who was severely scapegoated by her family. All of our usual efforts had no effect on the mother, who remained convinced that the child was the sole problem that needed fixing. Eleven-year-old Diane joined in the verbal battering as mother's ally. Finally Clara and I asked them to stand and demonstrate what we were hearing by pointing accusing fingers at Katie while she stood with fists raised. Diane started to point, then erupted in tears that were soon mirrored in the other two. For the first time we had succeeded in penetrating the walls of hostility, opening the way for them to acknowledge the pain each was feeling.

We often used *objects as metaphors* in treatment. One day in group Clara used the spoons on the dining table to demonstrate family relationships. Carmen, the oldest of ten children, complained that her younger sisters had always resented her but described her relationship with her mother as very close. Clara laid out twelve spoons in a row: two tablespoons representing the father and mother, a teaspoon that represented Carmen touching the mother tablespoon, and the other nine teaspoons lined up beyond Carmen.

She agreed that she had generally served as her mother's right hand, helping to raise the younger children. Clara pointed out her position, standing between the other children and their mother, possibly accounting for their resentment. Aware that the mother had died when Carmen was in her teens, Clara added, "And then mother died" and removed the mother tablespoon, leaving no one between Carmen and the feared father. Carmen, usually a hard-edged woman, burst into tears.

Since that initial incident, we have asked the clients to place the spoons themselves to show how they view their family relationships. Much thought goes into how to demonstrate distance (one spoon far removed from the rest), closeness (one spoon on top of another), and dominance (one spoon higher than the other). In family sessions, the differences in the perceptions of family relationships are starkly outlined in this exercise.

During a session with Caroline, a mother who had killed her baby, Clara noticed a box on the table. She suggested that Caroline must feel she was inside such a box with the lid closed, not able to get out nor to see through the darkness. Caroline agreed. This image became the means of assessing Caroline's state of mind in future sessions: "Are you in your box today? Can you peek out? Is the lid open, partly open, or shut?" Caroline was initially better able to identify her feelings through the metaphor of the box than when asked how she was feeling.

We became conscious of the *cues to the five senses* after a group of mothers described the smells that they remembered from childhood—mostly beer and urine. We decided to provide a sweeter bank of memories. The children fingerpainted with pudding. Our Christmas trees were live. We served freshly baked cinnamon rolls, and if we did not have rolls available, Marilyn occasionally put spice in the oven for the aroma. One day she had several people drop in while she made chicken soup. As she told it, their tension eased visibly.

Marilyn produced our Cedar House blanket when we sensed a parent at the edge or a child in need of comfort. She would envelop the trembling person, usually a woman, with the soft folds, providing not only the tactile sensation but a kind of containment of feelings that threatened to go out of control. Sometimes she put the blanket in the dryer for a moment to add to the sensation of warmth. When the parent felt better, we would discuss the relationship between a warm blanket and parenting and how a warm blanket could feel to a hurting child.

We acquired *batakas*, padded bats that were popular in the 1970s for the expression of aggressive feelings. Since we worked with people who had been violent, we made a rule that the batakas were not to be used on people but to hit furniture. Some children went to it with a vengeance, hitting the floor until they were exhausted. Some adults found them useful for draining their rage, but a mother who had killed her baby taught us that the batakas were not for everyone. Hanging on to her control by a thread, she refused to touch them. We concluded that she was right, that she knew she was not ready for the physical reenactment of beating.

The approaches we tried stemmed from the clients' input, from our life experience, and from our training. We always sought to bring intuition and the mind into partnership to broaden and define our work.

Chapter 13

A Family Study

Much of what we learned at Cedar House, we owe to Paula.

She and her husband, Fred, were referred to Cedar House by Children's Protective Services after their two-year-old daughter was hospitalized with burns on her feet. Both the child, Angela, and her four-year-old brother, Billy, had been placed in foster homes. Paula and Fred were arrested for child abuse, and she was placed on probation as the abuser.

Paula, age twenty-seven, came from a middle-class home, but no one would have guessed it by the looks of her at the time. She was obese, often dirty, and unkempt—in apparent rebellion against her middle-class upbringing. The family's apartment assaulted the senses, sometimes including dog feces on the floor.

Paula and Fred had previously been in treatment with several mental health agencies, none of which they considered effective. Paula had attended a discussion group on women's issues at a Parent-Child Center, where our friend Roland Summit had served as a consultant. He remembered her well as one who did not fit in with the group. The other participants were repulsed by her presence, not only by her appearance and odor but by her manner and her beliefs. For example, she was fascinated with the idea that the devil could inhabit a child.

She was eventually referred by the Parent-Child Center to the Long Beach Mental Health Department. Roland did not see her again for years but heard from those in the Department of Mental Health that she had made no progress there and was considered untreatable. A social worker with the Department of Children's Services told us that Paula was "a schizophrenic who should probably never have her children returned."

Fred's life was devoted to appeasing his wife to prevent her eruptions of rage. He initially indicated that he had not been ordered to receive counseling, and he had no intention of being involved. Clara worked hard to include him and to get him to think of intervening to protect his children. In his mind, she was much too powerful to be stopped while in a rage. He was afraid of her.

Paula's attitude was that she knew what she needed in counseling, thank you. Both parents were angry at the police, at Children's Protective Services, the court, her mother, the foster homes, anyone who had dealt with them. They agreed that they wanted their children returned but were convinced that the social worker was prejudiced against them.

To counter her controlling manner, Paula was informed at the intake that the staff, not she, would plan her treatment. She was assigned to the Monday group and Fred to individual weekly therapy sessions. They could see their children once a month, but the visits had to be monitored. We arranged rides for them to ensure their attendance. Clara did most of the transporting, but I took a few turns. The usual insensitivity of my sense of smell was a godsend when in a closed car with Paula, but even I had to hold my breath occasionally. Clara's strong faith must have sustained her on those rides.

Clara's faith also proved helpful in dealing with Paula's religious bent, for Paula listened only to Christian evangelists on TV. Her children were not allowed to watch any other programs. As a Catholic, she prayed to the Virgin Mary but also attended a charismatic church.

Asked for her early memories, Paula had a hard time recalling any before age ten. She knew her father had left the family while she was a baby. She had a stepfather during her teen years, but as she told it, her parents did not care where she was or what she did. She did recall being molested by an "old man" in her neighborhood and later by her stepfather.

Fred had experienced many changes in his childhood. His mother left his father and moved to California, taking him with her for a time. After living in a variety of households, including a foster home, he finally went with his father, whom he described as dominant and unaffectionate.

Somewhat slow in cognitive abilities and socially underdeveloped, Fred's individual sessions were slow going. He came across as stubborn, defensive, and sometimes unreasonable. He tended to withdraw in order to feel safe.

In the beginning Paula was overbearing in the group. She repeatedly complained of injustices done to her. When she became emotional or angry, she left the group and vomited, disgorging the tension through retching. We soon assigned her to individual therapy sessions with Clara.

Eight months after joining the group, Paula shared her inner world with us, something she had not done in any previous therapy. The only one to show up for the group that day, she revealed to us her "friends" who had been with her since childhood. As pieces of her early years came back to memory, she recalled feeling lonely and "weird." She developed imaginary friends to whom she talked, all of them named, each with distinct personalities. Rose, the stable one, was in charge of an entire cadre of helpers. There were two others, both women, who headed up other activities in her life. At times the people of her inner world fought. Paula explained that at Cedar House, as well as elsewhere, she sometimes conversed with her combative friends.

After this revelation, Paula often left the group and went to the bathroom where we could hear her as she tried to straighten out her troublesome friends. She was well aware they were not real people, but imagined figures who represented different parts of herself. Nonetheless, they served as her means of bringing order into her chaotic, painful life. One time she told Clara, "Marie says you should be firmer with me." Clara replied, "Tell Marie I'll do that."

After many months of treatment, we became acquainted with the children when Paula was allowed to bring them from the foster home to Cedar House for group. She had to get up very early—a major change from earlier habits—to catch the bus, but she managed to do so for months.

Billy, a very active four-year-old, jumpy and fearful, often pretended he was a dog. Like his father, he was slow to catch on and did not blend with the other children. In time Paula admitted to many instances of abusing him, including throwing him down the steps when he was ten months old. Angela, a beautiful little girl with blonde curls, did not relate to others easily but was obviously more comfortable with life than Billy.

Fred meanwhile attended the fathers' group. He asked many questions, rarely listened to others' responses, and never did achieve acceptance from the other participants. Later we tried without success to include Fred and Paula in the couples' group, hoping he might learn, like the others, that both parents had some responsibility when a child was hurt. Fred turned his head and said, "I won't listen to crazy talk like that."

When Paula ran out of the house to vomit, the hose that washed away the gunk became a symbolic part of her therapy, representing the cleansing of her inner self. But one and a half years after entering Cedar House, she relinquished this behavior after we saw her through an episode of full-blown rage.

We had learned that the social worker planned to recommend at the next court hearing that the children not be returned home. We were in accord at the time, fearing that her preoccupation with her inner world would keep her unavailable and unaware of dangers to her children. We anticipated, however, that this news would be devastating to her. The social worker agreed to deliver the news to her at Cedar House, where Paula could have support. We lined the walls with staff members and our volunteer psychologist, Larry Hanna.

Paula did indeed erupt in a rage. She pounded the chair. She shrieked at a pitch and volume that hurt my ears. She continued to scream for some time, finally subsiding in tears and exhaustion. As Clara offered her tissues, Larry clapped and said, "That was wonderful, Paula!" It was, for she had stayed in the room and used words, not vomit, to express her pain and frustration. From then on, she no longer vomited on our porch.

Incredibly, the judge at the court hearing set aside the social worker's and our recommendation. Interviewing the children in her chambers for a few minutes, she decided that Angela was in good shape and should go home while four-year-old Billy should remain in the foster home. Fred and Paula felt they had won a major victory over us and the system. The judge's order created problems, however, both for Angela, who returned to an unsafe home, and for Billy, who could not understand what he had done wrong to prevent his going home with his sister.

A few weeks later Paula brought some thoughts that she had written to Clara and me:

> Rage-root-low self-esteem . . . hurting my babies—desire to hurt me. . . . why?—I am no good, I can do nothing right, I set myself up to fail. I can not accept this, so I blame others. . . . It is my fault when the children get hurt (unexplained bruises). I may not physically hurt them, but I might as well hurt them. I hate myself so much and am so angry at myself, I cause them to be hurt. . . .
>
> It was totally my fault when the kids were taken away. I did not want them because I was not worthy to have them. Outwardly I wanted them back, but deep inside I was saying "Never give them back. Adopt them out." Why? Because I am not fit to be a mother. . . . Outside I was overjoyed to have Angela home. Inwardly I was screaming "No, NO, NO, I don't want her, I don't deserve her, I am too unworthy. I can't be trusted." This is difficult being honest with myself and you and God. . . . I need help. . . .

In the weeks following Angela's return, we saw Paula and the child five days a week, and Paula had telephone contact with Clara and Marilyn over the weekends. She expressed her own doubts about her ability to control her rage with Angela's demands for care and attention. We noticed bruises, bumps, and skinned knees on Angela. The explanation was always reasonable: "We ran to catch the bus and she fell." We used role-playing repeatedly with both Paula and Fred to acquaint them with how a child feels. We discussed the injuries with Paula and made reports to the social worker. We allowed Paula to give full verbal vent to her rage at Cedar House while setting a firm limit against any kind of hitting. Meanwhile, Fred was encouraged to act as a parent who protects his children—even from their mother, if necessary.

Paula became more comfortable with her mothering as Fred began to assume more responsibility for Angela's safety and intervened when Paula became too upset. Paula herself came to Cedar House when she felt her rage rising, using the program as a safety valve and as a place of protection. She later told us that if Cedar

House had not been there for her, Angela would be dead. We believed her.

One day Paula said with breathtaking simplicity, "Rage is when you want to hurt somebody." I recoiled, for I perceived myself as one who wanted to help, not hurt, yet I had experienced rage in my time. In one of those soul-stirring moments of recognition, I realized that in the *moment* of rage, I did have the urge to lash out. While I had not acted on the urge in the same way, she and I were not so far apart after all.

As the staff continued to encourage her, Paula lost some weight and bathed regularly. Roland Summit was surprised to see her at a statewide conference, a delegate of the PTA, standing in the audience to speak of her personal experience with child abuse. She had become an activist, confident and articulate enough to share her thoughts in public, a far cry from the misfit he had met at the Parent-Child Center. Billy eventually returned to his parents, leading us to keep close contact for another few weeks. There did not appear to be as much tension in this reunion as there had been in Angela's case.

Shortly after the family's termination, Clara wrote the following:

> After two years, the parents decided they no longer wanted to attend the various groups and sessions at Cedar House. Angela was placed in a daycare nursery known to Cedar House staff, and Billy was seen in a day treatment center—both children cared for by others who were aware of the abuse problems in the family. The family still drops by Cedar House occasionally, and there is warmth and concern for each other. Paula is still overweight, a little cleaner, able to converse, more aware, and a student at City College. Fred still struggles with his employment, but he is a caring father. . . . The house is only a little cleaner but smells better. Paula no longer needs to leave the room to talk to her imaginary friends. She is still domineering but can tolerate having someone who cares about her quiet her. Angela may need therapy later on. Billy remains in therapy. The family is aware there are those who care and will help. They know how to reach out in a more positive way to get what they need.

Years later we saw the family once more when the children were nine and eleven years old. Paula had maintained her weight loss. Both parents grinned from ear to ear and reminisced about the court hearing at which "Angela smiled so much at the judge that she let her come home." Angela shared their feeling of triumph. Billy was still rather awkward in his manner, but he and his father appeared to have an affectionate, teasing relationship, with most of the teasing done by Billy. Their situation was still not ideal, for Angela had reportedly been molested by their pastor, and the marriage was shaky. But Angela and Billy made it clear that they preferred life with their parents to a foster home. Both parents beamed.

Chapter 14

Crisis Intervention

To prevent a child from getting hurt when a parent felt stressed, we looked for ways to provide a supportive network that would be available at any hour. Marilyn or a trusted volunteer was on call for drop-in clients. We explored with the parents who among their families and friends would be available to them in a time of need. Each family had the Cedar House telephone number. Marilyn had Clara's number for backup, and those families in greatest need had Clara's home number as well. A few had my home number, although the other team members and I were more protective of my family life, given that I had three young children to raise.

We encouraged the parents to come or call if they felt they were in danger of hurting their children. For many of them, unaccustomed to trusting or reaching out, it was not easy at first to call on us. When they finally did, we welcomed the calls as a step toward growth, in some cases a giant step. Once they received the message that their calls were not only received but welcomed, some entered a new phase of making frequent calls.

Since we were dealing with many people to whom boundaries were not at all clear, even if expressed, we occasionally received calls in the middle of the night that had nothing to do with their children. It was not exactly endearing to wake up at 3:00 a.m. to hear,

> "Tony thinks he can just go out any time he wants and he doesn't think about me and now he's saying he doesn't care what I think and don't you think that he should . . . ?"
>
> "Are you afraid someone might get hurt?"
>
> "No, but—"
>
> "Where is the child?"
>
> "He's asleep."

"Then you two will have to deal with this yourselves for now. We can talk about this tomorrow. Be sure to call me."

Rather than becoming annoyed with them for interrupting our sleep (at least in our rational moments), we thought of this as another opportunity to teach appropriate boundaries. For the most part, they caught on rather quickly to when they truly needed to call and when they were expected to deal with problems on their own.

The telephone was our lifeline to families. Even those who had no phone would call from a neighbor's place or a pay phone in times of crisis.

We considered the training for volunteers who answered the phones to be as important as for those who worked in the groups. Clara wrote up a guide for those on the receiving end of a crisis call or greeting an upset parent who dropped in.*

* * *

Crisis. A crisis in Cedar House terms is an incident where the parent is in emotional overload (out of control or nearly out of control) and fears he or she will hurt the child. And in some cases, the call or drop-in does not occur until after the child is hurt.

CH crises always have to do with abuse or misuse of a child or children but always there is concern for the entire family, as child abuse is a family problem.

Objectives of the telephone answerer:

1. *Stay calm* (at least in voice), as the one calling is experiencing, along with others in the home, a chaotic, highly emotional experience.
2. *Speak softly but firmly,* be in control, as the caller is probably out of control, screaming, threatening, etc. The caller must feel that someone is in control at that point.
3. *Find out where the child/children are right at that moment.* Your focus must be on the safety of the child/children without

---

*Most of the crisis calls to Cedar House were initiated by mothers. This was probably because the majority of the children were in the primary care of their mothers. Although Clara wrote the guidelines relating to calls from mothers, the process applies equally to crisis calls from fathers.

in any way giving the parent the message he or she is not being heard. Some calming words such as, "I can really hear how upset you are. Now let's work together to get the child/children safe so we can really talk. You sure could use a few minutes all to yourself."

4. *So far you have concentrated on the parent. Now you can begin gently to question her as to where the children can be placed in the home so they can be safe and she can have time away from them.* You continue to concentrate on the mother and her needs but require her help in getting the children safe in the house and from her. This is the beginning of penetration of the emotional overload—the gentle questions regarding safety of the children require some thought by the mother.

5. Continue to concentrate on the mother by assuring her you will be right there at the phone while she removes the children from her presence in a place that you and she have worked out. You are still more of the control than she is. She is responding to your suggestion that the children be safely placed.

6. When she returns to the phone, she may need to tell you how terrible the children are, that she is going to give them back to somebody or other, and many other statements that are inappropriate for the so-called "responsible parent." Allow her to ventilate and respond with general kinds of statements; e.g., "Yes, kids can really push your buttons," or "It sure isn't easy to be a parent," or anything you have felt as a parent when it feels like kids are doing something to you.

7. Somewhere in this early phase—at least, any time after she gets the kids safe—the mother is encouraged to be good to herself by indulging in something that makes her feel better, perhaps a cup of coffee, tea, or a warm bubble bath. Ask the question, "What makes you feel better?" and suggest that she go make herself a cup of hot tea or coffee while you wait. This may or may not work at this point, but it does tune the mother in that you are concerned for her.

8. *As the parent talks out some of the abuses she feels from the children, her voice will change.* Look for those changes in voice and content. Your role is to really hear her distress and respond to her alone. For instance, "You know I had the same

feeling with my kids, and sometimes I tried. . . . Do you think that would help you any?" But keep such personal statements short and above all honest. As upset as this mother is, her antennae for phoniness is high.

9. *Tie-down time.* As you experience the change in voice and content, you may begin to be a little more specific in your questions; e.g., "It sounds like you have yourself in better control and are feeling a little better about your situation." If her response is negative, you might want to suggest she come to Cedar House or go visit a relative or friend. Or maybe she can call her friend to come over and stay a while. Attempt to make a plan with her for her own good and the children's safety. You must stay with her until a plan is arrived at and you have tied down the next step. Also at this tie-down period, you make arrangements for her to call you at such-and-such a time or you call her at a certain time. She and you will only feel safe if you have arrived at a concrete plan for the next contact—say in two hours.

Things that help in this kind of situation:

1. Common sense. You do not need to be a therapist to do this well. Some therapists cannot do it. Use your own life experience and draw on it.
2. Some kind of respect for the caller's ability to solve problems. You cannot solve them for her—just help her get free enough from her over-loaded emotions so she can think and plan with your help.
3. A gut feeling that parents do not want to hurt their kids but sometimes become frustrated and have little or no support system to help during that time.
4. Ability to focus on the safety of the child, which entails concentration on the feelings of the parent at crisis time.

Some things that can get in the way:

1. Telephonee too judgmental—thinking during the conversation that the parent should know better than that, she is acting like a child, etc.

2. Telephonee talks too much instead of allowing the parent time to get the emotional discharge out. Telephonee feels uncomfortable with silences or too much verbalization of parent.
3. Telephonee gets antsy that caller is not going to come up with any solution and so does not help the caller to work on the solution but presents the solution.
4. Telephonee too early makes the transfer of interest from parent to children. Early in the call, parent does not want to hear that the behavior of the children is normal for that age. She must be heard first and calmed down before any kind of rational thought can be introduced and dealt with. If you make such a statement before she is ready for it, she will feel you are rejecting her and siding with the children. The rule is—adult worked with first if child is to be safe.
5. Giving her control of situation too early.

If the child is hurt when parent calls, then the telephonee works to get the parent to take the child to the doctor. Honesty with the parent requires that at some appropriate time and appropriate place in the conversation it is noted that reporting child abuse to police is necessary. (Some of the words needed to approach this subject with the parent will be discussed.)

* * *

Occasionally a parent arrived with a child in tow, asserting an urge to harm the child. We took the parent's word for it, offered a cup of coffee, listened to the parent's story of the child's misbehavior and other immediate stresses, and looked for signs that our listening ear was relieving enough of the tension to assure the child's safety when they returned home. Before they left, we explored the parent's state of mind once again. Did she believe the child would be safe with her now? What safety valves were available to her? If the child misbehaved, how would she deal with it? Who would she call if she felt the tension rising again? Again, we took the parent's word for it if she still did not feel safe with the child.

In such a case (which was by no means frequent), we considered the need for respite care. We had several volunteers who took children into their homes for a night or two, and more than once I had one or two children at a time in my home on an emergency basis.

Marilyn welcomed children overnight at Cedar House, sometimes in a time of crisis, more often as a fun time for baking cookies or playing games.

If a night or two of respite care was insufficient and the parent still reported feeling dangerous, we broached the question of placement for the child and noted whether the parent responded with indignation or relief. If the latter, more often than not, placement was in order. Voluntary placement was not always easy to come by, but we kept close tabs on the family, sometimes daily, until the child was safely in another setting or until the storm passed.

It was our belief that a parent who called to report feeling the urge to kill was asking to be stopped and thus had already taken the first step to prevent harm. Almost always a calming voice sufficed to allay the crisis. When parents showed no signs of calming down, however, we either asked them to come to Cedar House for a respite or, more likely, we advised, "We're coming!" and made a home visit. One thing we did not do (although we could envision the need under certain circumstances) was to call the police when a parent made a threat against the child. A former client told us that after we left Cedar House, she tried calling an agency for help with her rage and was aghast to find the police at her door. Her trust shattered, she never called again. The child may have been protected in that moment, but, not having been harmed when the police came, he was left with his stressed mother, in greater danger through the loss of her safety valve.

When would we call the police in response to a threat? If a parent told of having a gun or another weapon, we would call the police before going ourselves. Fortunately for us, this never occurred on our watch.

I recall one night, however, when we made sure the police arrived before we did. On this occasion, well after dark, a nine-year-old boy appeared at our door, panting from having run more than a mile, to report between gasps that his stepfather had just kidnapped his younger brother. We called his mother, who had already called the police. Having no idea of the husband's intentions, we were not ready to enter the scene until we were assured that the police had arrived. Once we had that assurance, we went to lend what support we could.

The child returned home some two weeks later, deeply traumatized. But that is another story.

Chapter 15

Caroline

Caroline looked like a porcelain doll, beautiful and fragile. Caroline's tiny hands had battered her infant daughter to death.

When Caroline came to us, she had just returned from a three-month psychiatric evaluation at a prison. The court sentence required her to seek counseling. She and her husband, Steve, had already attended a few sessions with a psychiatrist, but her probation officer and her son's social worker were anxious that she be accepted into Cedar House.

The initial intake included Caroline, her husband, Steve, and her three-year-old son, Dale. The product of an interracial marriage, Caroline was striking in appearance with her dark hair and fine features. She wept with an air of helplessness through much of the intake. Steve came across as outgoing, solicitous of his wife, and openly grieving for his dead child. He had maintained the care of Dale during Caroline's incarceration, and the two had developed a close bond. During the intake we learned that Caroline had initially convinced an investigator that a stranger had broken into the house, tied her up, and beaten the baby to death. It crossed our minds that Paula would never have been able to sell that story. Caroline, with her tiny stature and helpless demeanor, succeeded—for a time.

Shortly after the intake, we met with others to consider whether Dale should be removed from the home until Caroline and Steve could put their lives together. The table was crowded, for in addition to the couple and the staff, the gathering included Caroline's probation officer, the family's social worker, and the psychiatrist.

Caroline's return to the home called for a change in the arrangement for Dale's care. All agreed the boy could not be left alone in his mother's care at this time. Both Steve and Caroline insisted that they were nonetheless able to look after him. According to the plan presented at the intake, Dale was to spend his days across the street with a neighbor until his stepfather came home from work and retrieved him.

The psychiatrist considered the plan viable. The social worker and the Cedar House staff considered it a terrible plan, foreseeing that the arrangement could create problems. Clara argued that we could not approve without having more idea of the mental condition and emotional state of the boy, the mother, and the father. Dale had lost his sister and then his mother. What had he seen? How much trauma was he dealing with, and how did he express it? Was this something the neighbor was equipped to handle? How much of her own guilt, mourning, and humiliation had Caroline dealt with? Would there not be resentment of Steve's close bond with Dale while this was not permitted to her? Would Steve unwittingly use the situation to assure that Dale remained his special boy, apart from his mother? How was Steve dealing with his own grief and anger at his wife? We considered it important to explore the dynamics of the death of the baby and be assured that the parents had dealt with their depression, their grief, and the causes of the situation before bringing Dale back into the home with the two of them. We did not consider reunification impossible, but we foresaw much work to be done to give the family a fighting chance for a good outcome.

Caroline, guilt-ridden, felt powerless to be other than an onlooker in the discussion. The psychiatrist argued that Caroline had never harmed the boy and that there was no need to keep them separated, given the precautions. The psychiatrist's view prevailed in Dependency Court.

Some three months later the situation became intolerable to all concerned. Seeing her son across the street without having daytime access to him aroused considerable resentment and guilt on Caroline's part, feelings she was not yet ready to handle. As he picked up Dale each day, Steve developed a fascination with the neighbor, a turn of events that became apparent to Caroline. Steve and Caroline were in marital and individual counseling with Clara, who was aware that all was not well in their household. When a social worker learned that the couple was fighting and that Steve sometimes left Dale alone with Caroline against the court order, the boy was placed in a residential facility many miles removed from Long Beach and his family.

Soon thereafter, Clara received a cordial phone call from the psychiatrist, asking for a bibliography on child abuse.

Caroline came faithfully to therapy and by court order attended the parenting class as well. Steve accompanied her at first, occasionally bringing Dale along before the boy was placed. Dale, understandably anxious, cried for his stepfather when in the playroom.

It was clear that the dead baby had not been unwanted, for both parents had welcomed the pregnancy and both hoped for a girl. Caroline had suffered from postpartum depression, however. She recalled, even in the hospital, telling her mother and Steve that she did not feel able to handle the baby at that point. They responded with reassurances that everything would be all right. She was not reassured. Once home with the baby and little Dale, she sometimes called Steve, asking him to come home. He did not. Caroline took the bruised baby to the pediatrician, hoping for help, but did not bring herself to ask for it. He saw the bruises but did not make a report. Caroline's father had been the more nurturing parent (though not always available), so she had learned to look to men for help, not to her mother. As the men she called on failed her, she felt totally isolated and overwhelmed, especially when the baby would not stop crying.

In joint counseling, Steve asserted that he loved his baby girl but did not blame Caroline for what she did. Caroline remained passive while Steve spoke for both of them. She wept but could not verbalize the feelings behind the tears. It took five sessions before Steve expressed any negative feelings toward Caroline.

When offered the batakas, Caroline refused to touch them, but Steve beat the furniture until he was exhausted. Caroline was repelled by his display of anger, which too closely mirrored her own rage that had gone out of control.

Clara asked Steve to take a look at what part he played in the family dynamics. Was he protective, treating Caroline as the fragile doll that she appeared to be? Did he gladly take on the role of strength in relation to her weakness, thus contributing unwittingly to her dependence and feelings of helplessness? Midway through the therapy, as Caroline became stronger and as Clara brought up uncomfortable questions, Steve stopped coming. Clara said she could not support Dale's return to the two of them unless Steve was included in the therapy. He refused. Caroline decided to separate from him, to find a job, and to work for the return of her boy. Her therapy continued.

She did some brave work. Aware of Caroline's tendency to arouse protectiveness among those around her, Clara offered empathy but gave her no slack in her therapeutic work. She demanded that Caroline recount in detail exactly how she had battered the baby. "How did you hold your fist? Where did it land? What did the baby do? Then what did you do?" These were not easy sessions for either of them.

Caroline found it difficult to hold a job in her state of depression. In time she began to miss appointments, particularly when she was informed that Cedar House's recommendation was that Dale remain in placement while she stabilized her life.

Cedar House staff made a home visit. In her own home, Caroline was better able to express her anger and show the depth of her depression. She was then able to see that as an adult she was following her little-girl habit of going to her room when she was hurt and angry. She was told that Cedar House would continue to recommend placement for Dale until she demonstrated the ability to reach out and ask for help when she needed it. We knew it was new to her to reach out, but for parents rearing small children, we saw this as a necessary safety valve.

Caroline missed a few more sessions, but then she requested a meeting of all agency representatives still responsible for her case. At that meeting she was no longer the porcelain doll but a woman, open and vocal, who intended to do what was necessary to get her son back. The Probation Department, the Department of Public Social Services, Caroline, and the Cedar House staff became a team. She was made aware of each agency's expectations.

Caroline visited Dale each week, driving two hundred miles to do so. Steve visited occasionally but grieved on his own without therapeutic help. Cedar House staff contacted him to encourage his return, but he stayed away.

The focus of Caroline's therapy was recognizing her rage, finding the means to defuse or control it, and looking at what made the difference in her treatment of her daughter and her son, whom she never harmed. We learned of many factors involved in the death of the baby: Caroline's rage at her mother, who would not allow her to express herself as a child or as an adult; her rage at her frequently absent father who, though loving, did not intercede when her mother hurt her; her mother's denial that there was any such thing as "mother's blues"; the baby's constant crying; rage at her husband who saw the baby's bruised face and said nothing; anger with authorities who did nothing when the baby was first hospitalized but returned the infant with minimal questioning; fear of that rage within her which she did not understand and felt she could not control, confirming in her mind that something was terribly wrong with her; guilt for not being able to please her parents as a little girl; and feelings of total helplessness. All these elements together culminated in the death of the baby.

When she felt strong enough to endure the experience, Caroline went to the grave for a final farewell, sobbing and repeating, "I am so sorry! I am so sorry!" She also went back to the pediatrician and spoke to the fact that he had seen bruises on the baby but had ignored them.* Not laying the blame on him, she took responsibility for the death, but wanted to alert him to what he could do in the future to prevent such tragedies.

At about this time, Clara and I attended a conference at which actress Florence Henderson spoke on behalf of Dale's residential facility. She gave a stirring talk about a little boy whom we recognized to be Dale. She told how the center had rescued him from his intolerable family and had provided him a place to heal. Clara was livid at the demonizing of his mother, as though only the residential center, not Caroline, had produced this nice child.

Scheduled to speak the same afternoon, Clara walked the halls to let off steam. That afternoon, speaking off the cuff as usual, she gave one of her most impassioned and moving talks.

At last, after many tears and much hard work on Caroline's part, Clara, the staff, and the social worker believed the situation was stable enough for Dale's return to his mother. In court, however, the residential facility was not in accord. All agreed that Caroline was ready for reunification, that she and her son had a very strong bond,

---

*Since then, the laws in California requiring doctors and others to report child abuse to the authorities have been strengthened and more widely emphasized.

and that Dale wanted to go home with her. Still their representative argued that Dale should finish school in their program where he had a richer environment than would be available to him in his home. We were appalled that the lavish physical setting was considered an argument to keep the family apart.

Dale, then five years old, came home. He also came often to Cedar House, sometimes spending time with Marilyn. Caroline remained on probation and continued with her therapy and the parenting class. Steve never did return to Cedar House. Eventually he and Caroline reconciled and received permission to move the family out of state, where they had another baby.

Clara and Caroline had occasionally talked of establishing another child abuse program in the dead baby's name, hoping to create a memorial to her short life and a means to prevent other such trage- dies. When Clara and I started Sarah Center in 1984, the dream came to pass. When Clara wrote Caroline of our plan, she wrote in reply:

> We received your letter . . . and were really glad to hear from you. To tell the truth it brought tears to Steve's and my eyes. Steve and I both agree for you to use Sarah House [our original proposal] as the name for your organization. Steve was very touched by the gesture. . . . If it can help but just one family, then it will be worth everything to us. We hope one day to be there to actually see it. I guess dreams can come true. I have often thought about Sarah House, but never thought it would be a reality. . . . I often think of Cedar House and everyone there. . . . Dale still thinks of you and Marilyn all the time. He misses Marilyn's cinnamon rolls and sleeping over. . . . The boys are fine. . . . Dale is still my Dale. So full of life and sunshine. . . . As for me, life is good and getting better each day. Once again, my friend, thank-you for the gift of Sarah House.

Not long ago Clara had occasion to contact Caroline, and the two of them had a long conversation. Caroline reported that the family was together, doing well, and that Dale, an adult now, was working with his father. On a trip to southern California, the family had visited the baby's grave. Following the visit, Dale had sobbed uncon- trollably in the car. We have wondered just what he remembers and what he knows. Perhaps one day he will tell us.

Chapter 16

Home Visits and Other Outreach

Cedar House could not have worked with the population we served, particularly those in the Monday group, without making home visits and outreach calls. As already noted, these were not families who were used to keeping schedules or who came readily for therapy.

The home visits served several purposes. Initially, we went to make contact with those who had no phones and to reduce their fear of coming into a new situation. In our ongoing work we frequently went to the homes of those who had missed group or appointments in order to maintain contact. One mother, whose life consisted of a series of crises, commented good-naturedly, "I might as well come because if I don't, they'll be at my door."

We were aware that people in depression may be immobilized, unable to rouse themselves to leave the house. If we suspected this to be the case, we went to them. Other times, when we feared for the safety of a child, we went to get a sense of the atmosphere in the home, to evaluate the parent's rage level, the degree of neglect, and to weigh the risk to the child. In our assessments we looked at such factors as the condition of the children, the condition of the house, and the reaction of the children to our appearance on the scene, as well as the parent's state of mind, available resources, and safety valves. Marilyn's presence had an especially calming influence on those who were on the edge of control. On occasion she was known to help a client do the dishes or clear off a table to provide one place where the eye could rest with a sense of order.

Some clients invited us to come. When we could find the time, we went, not only to reduce their isolation but also to provide them an opportunity to be the hosts. As they served us coffee in their living rooms, there was an equalizing effect. They not only had something to learn from us but they had something to offer us as well.

Home visits were not essential in every case, nor does every kind of therapeutic work require them. But where children are not safe, where domestic violence occurs, where people are overwhelmed with their rage and have no idea how to manage it, where people are immobilized by depression, effective treatment and the safety of the family calls for outreach in their homes.

As parents described incidents in their lives, it proved useful to be able to picture the situations in their settings. We learned that homes were not always as described, for some who described their homes as "a pigsty" proved to be good housekeepers, while in other households the reverse was true. We looked for various cues. Did the house reflect order, chaos, or something in between? What kinds of pictures were on the walls? Were there signs of a child's presence?

One mother expressed frequent disapproval of her six-year-old daughter Carrie, a slow learner in school. When I visited the home, I was struck by a visual overload in the living room, full of elegant glass and mirrors, reflecting light and motion, the walls covered with framed photos of the mother and various other people, mostly men. I did not see one photo of Carrie nor any hint that a child lived there until I went to Carrie's bedroom, a bleak room with a bed and a few toys, nothing more. I had been aware that the mother resented her daughter, but the home visit told me far more than her words how little Carrie was valued.

We became alert to the presence and the role of pets in the household. One little boy, Timmy, repeatedly crawled around the playroom on all fours and occasionally barked like a dog. In a home visit we became acquainted with the family's dog, which the parents presented with pride and affection beyond that they showed the child. We concluded that the dog's position in the family was more to be envied than the boy's. Small wonder that Timmy emulated the dog.

We developed a sense of eating patterns through our home visits. We could see if the child had a place at the table with the family. If the only eating place (a table or counter) was piled high, then the family members probably ate in front of the TV. One of the saddest children in our experience was an eight-year-old boy who was banished to the kitchen to eat alone while his parents shared their meals in front of the TV in the living room.

We rarely went alone on a home visit, usually going in twos or threes, bringing our complementary skills. We found we received more information and impressions from several pairs of eyes. One of us would talk with the mother (and father, if available) while another would relate to the child. A third person might be involved with another child or a grandparent. If the family members were not especially needy that day and could share their time, we would sit together, focusing on the family interaction rather than on the individuals.

We never knew exactly what to expect on a home visit. Occasionally we found ourselves in ludicrous situations. Pam and I went to talk with a man, Tony, who had been accused by his girlfriend of leaving a bruise on her child. The girlfriend invited us in, but Tony had retreated to the bathroom. We conducted an interview through the bathroom door, Tony refusing to come out but conversing from within. We stressed that we were not associated with the police, that we were there to help if there was any way we could, and that we assumed he had not set out to hurt the child but found his anger getting the best of him. He concurred. After a half-hour or so, Tony shouted, still through the bathroom door, "I like the way you guys work!" Standing in the hallway, shouting back, I restrained my impulse to laugh aloud. We never did see his face that day, but the child received no more bruises.

After Cedar House was chosen as a model for Los Angeles County's Neighborhood Family Centers, we argued the need for home visits among the services to be offered by the centers. Some said this required too much staff time. We replied that too many suffering people and too much information were lost without home visits. In recent years we have been gratified to learn that some county officials, including members of the Interagency Council on Child Abuse and Neglect, have asserted the need for home visits in the effective treatment of child abuse. The county's current Family Preservation Project provides services in the home with the participation of Sarah Center.

Among families with telephones, we had another avenue of outreach. Those who did not show up for a session received calls to see if they were okay. We listened for signs of depression (a monotone, flat expression, hopelessness) or for a rising rage level. Either could signal the need for a home visit.

Pam provided outreach for the children by arranging to spend time with those who seemed particularly needy. Sometimes she or a volunteer took a child out to experience "the softer side of life," perhaps at the beach or in a petting zoo. A favorite place was a hat shop where the child had an opportunity to try on all kinds of hats in front of a mirror. Some children, convinced they were ugly and unacceptable, had a hard time looking at their own images at first, but Pam's good humor overcame their reluctance. The fact that she was pleased with what she saw in them helped them to take a look at themselves through her eyes.

Without the outreach of home visits, telephone contacts, and occasional outings, we believe that the therapeutic work with this population would not have continued nearly as effectively—and in many cases, not at all.

Chapter 17

Transportation

With our experience of working with people in poverty, we figured from the beginning that we would have to arrange transportation to get some of them to group.

Sometimes we found the families ready and willing to go, while other times they had overslept or were unsure whether they wanted to go that day. We learned to stand and wait without advising while they tried to make up their minds. They generally decided to come. Sometimes, though, we set limits on entering the car with overflowing coffee cups or sticky peanut butter sandwiches.

Clara arranged to pick up Helen, her boyfriend Sam, and three-year-old Jimmy each week. It was not unusual to find them still in bed. One day they clearly did not want to come to group, but they could not bring themselves to say so. Jimmy allowed Clara to dress him while his parents hemmed and hawed. Finally, reluctantly, they followed Clara to the car where, as it happened, she had a donated rocking horse in the back.

"So where would you rather go?" Clara asked, acknowledging the family's reluctance.

"Disneyland!" they responded.

"Let's go!" said Clara. "What's your favorite ride?"

The family had a wonderful time en route to Cedar House, sharing a fantasized trip to Disneyland. The rocking horse became the carousel. When the car lurched, it became a roller coaster. By the time they arrived, late for group, they were all in high spirits, Clara included. The group asked where they had been. Helen and Sam both replied, "Disneyland!" and grinned with the enjoyment of their in-joke.

While at Cedar House, Clara wrote up her thoughts on transportation:

The Use of the Automobile as a Vehicle

In our program team members transport group members to group meetings and to the doctor, mental health agencies, etc. The automobile comes to represent Cedar House and is important because breaking isolation is one of the goals for the families. The car is a bridge between home and Cedar House, between home and the outside world.

To get a family to group, it works best if the same person in the same car picks up the same family week after week. This establishes the needed sense of continuity.

When the driver knocks on the door, this person has a first-hand view of what is going on in that family. The mother or child (sometimes the father) pours out problems of immediate concern. You are the first on the scene. Be aware of the care of the home and how prepared the family is for going to Cedar House. If the parents state they are not coming today, do not hurry off, but listen and respond. Many times parents will state they are not going, but as they talk, they decide to go. The point is not to press them to go but listen to where they are. This often frees them to go.

The automobile represents many things to the passenger. It represents continuity by showing up at a specified time each week. This gives a sense of a stable happening in an otherwise unstructured life. As the driver becomes acquainted with the family, the parent may look forward to seeing a friend, someone who cares. The children look forward to getting into "the blue car" or whatever. The driver may personalize the car in a fun way by calling it "Ms. Blue," or whatever name fits. The car and driver can represent a play time for both parent and child. The responsibility for getting some place (after all are ready) is in the hands of the driver.

The car is a small enclosed place; the driver and passenger do not face each other. This intimate setting plus the side-by-side seating arrangement offers a nonthreatening kind of setting. Often the parent feels free to talk about very intimate things, the current crisis in the family. The children also offer insights to the listener during this drive.

If the parent is shy about asserting herself in the group discussion, the driver (as a team member in the group) may, as appropriate, help the parent. The driver may listen for an opening and say something like, "Isn't what Diana is saying something like you were telling me in the car?" The driver thus supports the parent to share with the group, to take part. The danger of this method is that the parent may become dependent on the driver to bring him or her into the group. The driver must be sensitive to this and prime the situation only until the parent can handle entry into the group process. If the parent gives no response to the driver's attempt to get him or her into the group, the driver can wait and try again another time.

Having different types of items in the car can be valuable for both the parent and the children. In the course of using your car, you may have articles in it. Do not feel you must remove them, for they can bring interest and new experiences to the family. One need not call attention to them. The families will see and perhaps touch as they get free to do so. If children have found articles of interest, they are excited to get in the car to see what they may find.

The car should be a happy place, a fun time. One goal with parents is that they learn to play, as often they have not learned to do so in their childhood. A light mood is sure to occur if the driver makes a wrong turn and makes a playful comment about it. The parent can identify with the driver as a person who can make mistakes and also sees another way of handling being in the wrong. The driver can add to the effect on the next ride by mentioning that she hopes she can turn the right way this time.

A particularly isolated parent may feel uncomfortable in the car for a few weeks. In such a case, the driver stays with very safe subjects, waiting for the parent to feel safe enough to share. The noise of the motor offers a type of protection to parents who find it difficult to talk when everything is quiet. Perhaps the fact that there is movement gives some sense of satisfaction to the otherwise isolated parent who usually stays in the same place all the time—it feels good to be moving, even if it is only in an automobile. And perhaps moving in the automobile with a listener gives a boost to movement in personal development.

Chapter 18

Advocacy

Our practice of accompanying the more fearful clients or those without transportation to places they needed to go provided me with some of my most memorable eye-openers.

I had worked in a county agency. I had referred people elsewhere and figured I had done my job. I had no idea what my referrals entailed, however, until I went with the families.

Theresa, a mother suffering from schizophrenia, had two small children, no car, not even a stroller. The eighteen-month-old spent most of her days passively sitting in a playpen and had not yet attempted to walk. She was a heavy child, a load to carry any distance. The nearest bus stop was three blocks away.

Concerned about the children's development, we referred the family to the Department of Mental Health's Therapeutic Nursery, a program that we respected for its work with preschool children. Since they provided a van to pick up their clientele, we counted on their having the children five days a week. First, however, the children had to be evaluated and accepted.

I arranged to provide transportation for the intake interview. Theresa was nervous but trusted me enough to come.

When we arrived at the facility, we found the front door barred due to construction. There were no signs to indicate an alternative entrance, but with perseverance we found a side entrance leading to the Therapeutic Nursery.

When we arrived, there was no one to greet us. We waited while Theresa became more and more anxious. Finally a staff member, whom I knew and respected, emerged, took the older girl (age three) by the hand, and led her away without a word to the mother! I was flabbergasted. Theresa was agitated. It was all I could do to keep her from deteriorating on the spot.

Eventually, the intake completed, the older child was accepted but not the younger one, who was too young for the program. Theresa was told to go to another floor to arrange the fees. We obeyed, only to be told that she would have to make an appointment for another day. The child would not start in the program until the financial arrangements were complete.

I provided transportation again the following week. When we returned, however, the person with whom she had had the previous appointment had called in sick. Theresa had a phone, but no one had called to let her know. Had I not been available, she would have hauled a heavy baby several blocks to the bus, two more blocks after leaving the bus, only to find she had to come back yet another day. Her child would not have made it into the program if I had simply referred her and left it at that. I had a strong reaction to the experience, and I did not start out paranoid. We concluded that a person had to be pretty healthy to make it into the Department of Mental Health.

We spoke with the staff of the Therapeutic Nursery to describe the intake experience from the client's point of view. Thereafter they arranged for fees to be set the same day as the intake interview. Theresa's child went on to show dramatic improvement in behavior and development while in their program.

Going to court with families was another eye-opener. Although we were subpoenaed from time to time, we usually went primarily to provide moral support for the parents and for the children when they, too, had to be there.

Ruth had to go to court soon after Cedar House opened. Her public defender showed little interest in her case until Clara spoke on her behalf. At that point, it seemed to us, he began to represent her in earnest. This happened quite often.

I went to court with a young woman, Lily, who was scared and depressed. She sat with her head down and shoulders hunched. When her lawyer approached us, he addressed me, not her. It struck me how easy it is to overlook frightened people. Lily was later ordered to undergo a psychiatric evaluation and was diagnosed as "borderline retarded." We had seen her in our safer setting and knew she was nowhere near retarded. She must have been paralyzed with fear during the evaluation, a condition that apparently escaped the evaluator's attention. She did tend to have a blank expression when scared, possibly leading the evaluator to assume there was nobody home.

Parents who had a child removed from their home following an injury were terrified of taking a child to a doctor thereafter. One day a mother brought a feverish child to Cedar House. We recommended that the child see a doctor, but the mother could not bear to take him, fearing she would again be seen as unfit and the child would again be removed. Finally, when Marilyn promised to go with her, she reluctantly agreed. It turned out the child had an ear infection, and the doctor even remarked that the mother did well to bring the child when she did. She received much-needed validation; the child received the necessary medical attention; and the mother learned that her fear, grounded though it was in past experience, did not relate to current reality. We later made use of that realization as she dealt with other fears.

Sometimes we found ourselves in strange situations when we accompanied clients. Cedar House staff recommended that Helen's parental rights be terminated and that her daughter be put up for adoption after too many years in foster care. Helen had no transportation to go to court, but she was adamant that "No one's going to take my kid away from me!" As the court date approached, she asked Clara to drive her and her boyfriend, Sam, to the courthouse in Los Angeles. Clara and Marilyn agreed to go. There the two pairs sat on opposite sides of the courtroom, argued opposite sides of the case, then met for the long drive home. Oddly enough, Helen and Sam appreciated their presence, even though the child was ultimately put up for adoption.

Many of the families who came to us had had contact with the police. From the beginning we heard horror stories of how the parents were treated by police officers, most of whom they knew by name and by reputation.

We believed that the more a parent was humiliated, demeaned, or trivialized by those in authority, the more risk there was to the child when they were reunited, for the parent carried still another drop in a sea of self-loathing. We also knew that most children who were placed eventually returned home, and that most longed to be with their parents, abuse notwithstanding. (We always listened closely to those who did not want to go home.)

Clara became an advocate in earnest the day Ruth searched frantically for her missing child. When Ruth called the police for help, she learned that a police officer had removed the boy from their fenced front yard without notifying her. Her fury surpassed even her relief at finding that little Kevin was safe.

When Ruth was called in for an interview by a female officer in the Child Abuse Unit, the one who had removed Kevin from the yard, Clara decided to go with her. Officer Jackie Hammond had a reputation among the mothers as a tough, hard-boiled woman who gave no slack. In the course of their meeting, however, Clara spoke to both Ruth and Officer Hammond with respect for them and their immediate goals: Officer Hammond's, to ensure protection for the child, and Ruth's, to have her child with her. Officer Hammond spoke firmly of her expectations for the care of the boy, but she maintained a tone of respect. The child came home. Ruth attributed the civility to Clara's presence.

Later, Clara had occasion to accompany another mother, Marie, to Officer Hammond's office. After giving Marie a stern warning about protecting her children, Officer Hammond lent the incredulous woman money to feed those children.

This "hard-boiled" officer attended more than one of our group sessions, inviting dialogue. All in the group came to respect her commitment to the care of children. At the same time we noticed a change of tone in the Child Abuse Unit.

In the group, too, we noticed a change of tone. Ruth spent a brief term in the women's jail after she decided to serve the time on an outstanding warrant for drugs. When she returned, she remarked, "I never thought I would see the day that I would defend the police, but there I was, telling the others in jail that the police have a job to do!"

Unfortunately we continued to hear horror stories from parents whose children were picked up by the "black-and-whites," the officers on patrol who were not assigned to the Child Abuse Unit. We also had occasional dealings with the Los Angeles County Sheriff's Department and other nearby police departments.

One day we made a child abuse report to the Norwalk Police Department after we learned that a father in our program had molested his oldest daughter. Both parents were present as Clara called the police, and the entire family waited together for their arrival. When a policeman showed up to make the arrest, Clara objected to the children's father being handcuffed in their presence, arguing that the humiliation of the father would add to the trauma for the children. The policeman was stunned.

When I emerged from an individual session, I found the parents, looking scared but resigned, at the dining table with Clara, and the four children with Marilyn and Pam in the living room. I overheard the policeman as he reported over the telephone, "They won't let me handcuff him!" Several calls later, the policeman allowed the father to drive his own car to the police station. At this point *we* were stunned. We were relieved to learn that all went well, for the father dutifully followed the police car to his arrest.

We met numerous caring people in the system: Janice Wills, the adoption worker who counseled the parents considering relinquishment; the social worker who successfully fought in court for the protection of a child in a situation that the judge had trivialized; the compassionate county counsel who was delighted when we concluded that a child did not need to be in the system. But there was also the social worker, apparently going through a crisis of his own, who responded with total irrelevance to every statement that a mother made, until she turned to me and said, "He's not hearing me, Bobbi!"

The process of walking beside clients as they negotiated that which was required of them taught us a great deal. We discovered obstacles in their way that we had not imagined. We became more finely attuned to the families' fears that interfered with their abilities to get their needs met and that too often were interpreted as "resistance." We also became attuned to the local agencies' personnel as we met them in action, and we became better acquainted with the strengths and limitations of other organizations. We found ourselves modeling to clients how to face fears and overcome obstacles. If nothing else, we could at least validate for the clients that the mountain they had to climb, while not insurmountable, was not an easy one.

Chapter 19

Socialization and Empowerment

When Larry Hanna, our volunteer psychologist, joined us, he commented in amazement, "Do you know what you are doing here? You're socializing these people!"

In the groups, particularly in the Monday group, the process of socialization was gradual. Most of the parents initially came with undeveloped skills in relating to others. At times the competition for attention was keen among the talkers, especially when one was in the middle of a crisis that took up the group's time. We did not try to control who spoke when but gently invited other less vocal participants to share a similar experience or respond to what was said. ("Is what Marie described anything like what you went through, Linda?") If the parent chose not to speak, that was accepted, for we trusted the need to be heard to turn the tide eventually.

We arranged occasional parties and picnics that included staff, clients, and volunteers. In our experience this did not endanger the professional relationship but enriched it. Given a staff that was comfortable with inner boundaries ("Thou shalt not abuse others nor allow yourself to be abused") and whose needs for intimacy were met elsewhere, we could allow others, including our clients, to see us as social as well as professional individuals. We could have a good time together. In later years we were joined by recreation therapist Susan Mathieu, who was skilled at planning outings that offered opportunities for play.

While our primary purpose in such gatherings was the socialization of the families, we found material for therapy as well. One mother's overcontrolling style of parenting was glaringly evident as we hiked a nature trail. A father's determination to terrorize a volunteer with a lizard gave us a different view of him, lending credence to his daughter's allegation of sexual molestation. Until then we had not had as a clear a picture of his lack of empathy for others' feelings.

We thought of Cedar House as the clients' program as much as ours. Who better to speak to their needs? When visitors arranged to come, we usually invited some interested parents to join us for the discussion and the tour of the house. The visitors gained a more personalized view of the program, while the clients had a chance to interact with others in the community. Here they could be the experts. Rather than damaging their self-esteem by being associated with a child abuse program, such experiences proved to have the opposite effect.

While we offered a wide range of therapeutic activities at Cedar House, we did not try to restrict the clients to our program. We referred them to other agencies or, if they were already involved elsewhere, we usually encouraged their continuing. We had cross-referrals with the Department of Mental Health, Psychiatric Clinic for Youth (now the Child Guidance Center), Family Service of Long Beach, Navy Family Services, Catholic Welfare, Alcoholics Anonymous, Parents Anonymous, and others. As other twelve-step programs have developed since then, we have made referrals to them as well.

To avoid fragmentation, we tried to stay in touch with those providing services in other settings (obviously with the knowledge and consent of the clients). If a parent claimed to have received a contradictory message in another program, we called to ask if the client had heard them right and if so, to determine whether we were working at cross-purposes or toward the same end. Usually the clarification of each of our goals was sufficient to allay the client's confusion. Rarely did we find a therapist who expressed the wish to be the sole service provider, in which case the parent had to choose which path to follow. With multiproblem families, however, most of us recognized that we all benefited from the clients' broader involvement in the community and from the pooling of our talents.

Since many of the families felt out of place in the wider community, we brought the community to them—in the groups, in our open houses, and other events. Because many of the parents had had contact with the police, we suggested that we have a member of the

Child Abuse Unit of the Long Beach Police Department come to sit with the Monday group. This required preparation, for the mothers protested, some with jutting jaws, "I'm not coming to see no cop!" To their credit, they came—without exception.

Sergeant Bostard, who came out of uniform, was a good-looking man with a pleasant demeanor. He explained the mission of the Child Abuse Unit: to protect children who had been abused or were in danger of abuse. The mothers not only accepted but approved of this mission, particularly in light of their own backgrounds. ("Where were you when we needed you?!") At the same time they told how it affected them not only to have their children removed from them but to be treated like dirt in this wrenching moment. Sergeant Bostard acknowledged that the removal of a child could be done in a humane manner, while maintaining the necessity at times of the removal of a child pending an investigation. It proved to be a fruitful dialogue. We acknowledged the courage that it took for everyone— the outnumbered Sergeant Bostard as well as the mothers—to sit together at the same table.

When we suggested encounters with members of the police force thereafter, we met with little resistance from the groups. Officer Jackie Hammond (now retired) came more than once, following the meeting with Clara and Ruth. She recently remarked that she also felt a need for Cedar House: "I needed a place to vent the sorrow" from handling so many hurt children. As the mothers became more aware of her pain and she of theirs, a foundation for empathy was established.

Sometimes the community came to us unexpectedly. During our first summer, a volunteer organization offered to take the Cedar House children to the Los Angeles Zoo. We arranged a meeting of the planners with the parents, who liked the idea but made it known that they had never been to the zoo themselves. The outing became a family affair, and all had a wonderful time. The following year, we learned that one of the children advised a friend, "You should get into Cedar House. They go all kinds of neat places in the summer." His "all kinds of neat places" had consisted of one trip to the zoo.

We were always mindful of building relationships at Cedar House on a foundation of staff integrity and honesty. This meant, as situations came up, calling it as we saw it, gently perhaps but always truthfully. This provided a kind of security for the clients, who could spot anything phony.

For instance, a mother might report resentfully, "You know what my social worker said? She said I should move!" Clara, who was familiar with the home, would respond, "Yes, I can see how she might say that" and then start sorting out the sources of both the client's and the social worker's concerns. Was there a real risk to the child or the family? If so, what could be done to reduce the risk? "Maybe your worker didn't say it the way she should have, but I've had some concern myself about your situation. Let's take care of this and get the social worker off your back!"

However, if, after the sorting-out process, it seemed to us that the social worker had overreacted or been unfair, we might say, "That doesn't seem right to me either." The focus then turned to the question of how to proceed. "Could you call the social worker to find out what she expects? What do you need to say to her? I know that's what you'd *love* to say, but can we tone it down! Mainly you want her to know that—what? Let's try role-playing this conversation. . . . Okay, here's the telephone. You might as well call now while your message is fresh in your mind. If the social worker isn't there, you can leave a message that you want to talk with her. . . . Good for you!" In group, this process was usually accompanied by laughter as others offered what to say before all agreed on more acceptable terminology.

We were working, after all, with adults who needed very concrete guidance. We walked them through the process of identifying what part of the anger and hurt the alleged victimizer had caused and how much stemmed from their own actions or their long-held view of others as inevitable victimizers. ("Unless you have reason to know otherwise, remind yourself: 'This person is not here to hurt me.'") We went on to establish whether there was a need that required action and, if so, how they could proceed. Sometimes we needed to show them how.

We always validated their views when we could do so honestly. We made the assumption that what they described to us was what they believed and felt, even if it contradicted what we believed and felt. We did not deny what they told us, no matter how strange to our ears. We might say, "That's not the way I see it, but I know you have reason to see it the way you do." We did not focus primarily on their pathology but sought to nurture their strengths, their struggles, and their urge to make sense of their world.

We were not constrained by a diagnosis that, while helpful for providing a signpost for treatment, could also lead to false assumptions. In Paula's case, we were told she was a schizophrenic who should never have her children back. As we worked with her, we concluded she was certainly narcissistic but not schizophrenic.

Giving people permission not to be perfect proved a powerful means of empowering them to risk actions that they would never have attempted in the past. We often told them they were welcome at Cedar House, whatever their moods. Like any of us, they found it easier to feel good when they had permission to feel bad—i.e., real. We were tested at times by those feeling hostile, but I was always amazed at the power of acceptance to defuse bad feelings.

Staff members in a child abuse agency need to become comfortable enough with their own capacity for rage to be unafraid of others who have been violent. When a person arrives in a state of anger and a staff member responds in fear, the signal received by the client is "Sure enough, I am a scary, terrible person," which is at best a confirmation of a poor self-image and at worst an invitation to lash out. We leaned toward those who were on the edge of exploding, signaling our acceptance of their presence and our expectation that they would control their behavior in our presence. At the same time, of course, we communicated with our words and manner that we recognized their anger, that we were ready to hear them, and ready to deal with whatever problem was plaguing them in the moment.

Clara and Marilyn made a home visit with a father who they knew had inflicted brain damage on his child. Not knowing what they would find, they enlisted another father, a client, to join them, mostly for his male presence but also to speak to the experience of attending Cedar House.

The man proved to be large and intimidating. Clara is a small person but not one to be intimidated. As they talked, she spoke in her kindly way, moving toward him, bit by bit. He moved back, bit by bit, and finally dropped the attempts to intimidate. They could talk together as fellow human beings. He came to Cedar House soon after, moving toward us that time, taking a step toward socialization.

Chapter 20

The Parenting Class

Cedar House served parents with severe deficits in parenting skills. We saw the need for sessions on parenting, but our experience told us that many of our clients would not attend the classes available at the local colleges. We looked for a course at a more basic level in a nonthreatening atmosphere.

In May 1977 Long Beach City College (a two-year community college) and Cedar House joined efforts to start a twelve-week parenting class one evening a week, located in the informal ambience of Cedar House. City College hired a teacher, Carol Wollen, a specialist in child abuse and parent education, while Cedar House provided the services of Marilyn and a parent volunteer as coleaders in the adult group, as well as Pam and several volunteers to look after the children.

The classes were designed to meet the needs of a broad population, some court-ordered to attend, others referred by the Department of Public Social Services, community health and mental health agencies, parental stress groups, and educational institutions. Some found the class through brochures or word of mouth. Carol and Marilyn found that the mix of high- and low-stress parents was beneficial to all as long as the class leaders were sensitive to the special needs of the high-stress families. The commonality of parenting provided the bonding material for the mixed class.

Initially the plan was to limit the class to twelve to fifteen parents, but the requirements of Long Beach City College called for larger numbers. At the time of an evaluation of the program in 1979, the parenting class had eighteen participants, including nine Cedar House parents (six mothers and three fathers).

The goals of the class reflected the philosophy of both Cedar House and Carol, who proved to be a good match:

- To provide psychological support of parents' emotional needs in an environment that helps them to vent negative feelings freely, to become more responsive to resource help, and to accept themselves as people of value.
- To create opportunities for the parents to socialize and to develop a "family network" with one another for mutual support.
- To provide information on child development and positive disciplining techniques that are alternatives to physical punishment.
- To foster "mutuality" through pleasurable mother-child interaction, which is believed to be critical to the child's optimal development in areas of socialization, emotional health, and learning.

The class presented (in Carol Wollen's words) "an eclectic array of information drawing from current child development, behavioral (child management), humanistic, and parent effectiveness literature training." The parents began by identifying a target behavior, either in themselves or in the child, that they wanted to see change. The class then presented a sequenced program that led parents step by step, building practical knowledge and manageable skills. Based on the Systematic Training for Effective Parenting (STEP) program, the curriculum first presented the easier, more basic skills, assuring the parents that they would master each level before proceeding to the next step.

The first half of class time was reserved for parents' venting of feelings and discussions of problems that had arisen during the week. The students indicated that it was helpful to relieve the emotions that had built up during the week, making it easier to be receptive to the second half of the class time, when information was given and techniques discussed.

The first six weeks were geared toward information and skill building that would ensure the physical safety of the child: anger control techniques (words to use, physical exercise, mental exercises, walking away until cooled down, reaching out for help, etc.) and alternatives to physical punishment (time out, natural consequences, behavior modification, etc.). The content of the second six weeks concentrated on child-development information (what to expect at what stages) and building empathetic interaction and communication skills.

At the end of the class, the parents reviewed the target behavior to evaluate whether they were aware of any change. All who finished the course received certificates. Some of the parents, who had experienced little success in the past, cried when they held the tangible acknowledgment of their achievement in their hands.

In July 1979, there was an attempt to evaluate the success of the parenting class. In her two years of conducting the class, Carol Wollen had developed her own technique with the targeting of specific behaviors. Progress was to be measured by the increases or decreases in the targeted behavior. Unfortunately, shortly before the class was to begin, Carol became seriously ill and was unable to begin the class. Her replacement did not have time to learn Carol's training model and assessment techniques before stepping in.

Trying to construct tests regarding knowledge of parenting techniques and on very short notice, the instructor put together twelve true-false questions, six dealing with each topic. Fourteen students took the pretest the second night of the class. Twelve students took the posttest eight weeks later, but they circled both responses for several questions, not due to a misunderstanding, they explained, but as a result of what they had learned in the class. They could no longer respond to the test questions in terms of absolutes, for, depending on the circumstances, both response choices could be considered correct. For example, one question dealt with the immediacy of discipline. In general, disciplinary action should be taken as soon as possible after the inappropriate behavior has occurred. For parents who have problems controlling their tempers, however, discipline should be delayed until the parent has calmed down and thought the situation through.

The evaluation concluded, "Despite this problem in test construction, both parents and the instructor felt the students had gained a lot by the discussion of why certain questions could be considered both true and false. While no objective data was gathered regarding what students had learned thus far in the parenting class, the subjective responses indicated that the students felt they had benefited a great deal from the course."

The students' comments were all positive, indicating that self-control, self-esteem, and improved parenting skills were the major benefits of the class. Some written examples were as follows:

- "I have learned how to curb my temper, and it has made a great difference in the way my children behave."
- "Learning that my child's self-esteem is very important to him, and to learn to respect this right and not abuse it."
- "I have found that there are many ways of handling problems and situations with children and that provoking or encouraging a power struggle is futile, time-consuming, and hard on the nerves."

Parenting classes at Cedar House have continued to this day under various leaders. In my current private practice, I continue to meet parents who have attended the class. The reports continue to be positive.

Chapter 21

The Volunteers

A remarkable corps of volunteers provided the means to extend our program. Many were from the Junior League, an organization of women who raised funds and offered their talents to several programs in the area. Others found us through college classes, newspaper reports, or word of mouth.

All those interested in becoming volunteers attended an orientation session and five sessions on effective communication skills and sensitivity training. All completed an application that requested information on their background, interests, and preference for assignment. They received a *Volunteer Manual* that outlined the history and philosophy of Cedar House and provided information regarding what could be expected when dealing with abused children and their families. The manual listed some of our expectations:

1. Since staff models responsibility, it is imperative that you be on duty at your designated time and on time. If you cannot be here, call as soon as possible and let Cedar House know.
2. What goes on at Cedar House needs to stay at Cedar House. It is confidential. If you need to talk about it, do it with Cedar House people only.
3. If you are personally not in good shape, and nobody is all the time, let staff know.
4. If you choose to be in a therapy group, it will be necessary for you to attend staff meetings.
5. You will be busy at Cedar House doing whatever needs to be done at the moment—dishes, calls, etc., but sometimes you will just sit, so relax and do it.
6. It is important to share information and observations about a family. Whatever you bring is important, and you may have

part of the whole picture. Do not carry it alone. You will be a part of our team.

7. You will be expected to listen, with your outside as well as inside ear. Sounds easy? Not really.

There was a job for every talent. The primary volunteer assignments and those most coveted were assistants in adult groups, children's groups, parenting class, and general house coverage, the last of which included answering telephones, receiving visitors, chatting informally with clients who dropped in, and possibly washing the accumulating dishes.

Those volunteers who helped in our adult and children's groups were required to attend the weekly staff meeting, both to assure that we were all working in concert and also to give us another view of the families and the program through their eyes. Volunteers who answered the phones were encouraged to come to staff meetings, especially in the beginning of their service. We stressed the importance of a desperate client's first contact with the agency, given this clientele of people who had such a hard time reaching out for help. We were careful to find volunteers with welcoming voices, screening out those who were merely efficient.

Because some volunteers attended our staff meetings, they participated in our brainstorming and took on more responsibilities. We provided them the same kind of support and allowance for mistakes that the paid staff provided for each other. At the same time, we could be alert to problems as volunteers went out on their own. A male volunteer became sexually attracted to one of the clients. To his credit, he let us know, and potential problems were averted.

We operated on the premise that whoever had strong feelings about the need for a course of action was the appropriate one to pursue it, once all had agreed. This led some volunteers into territory they had not anticipated. A member of the Junior League found herself in a bar in a rough part of town, seeking a young mother who worked there. As she told it at the next staff meeting, "Can you just see me, walking in with all those tattooed men drinking their beer! I just put on my best swagger and asked for Jennifer." She found the woman, delivered a message, came to no harm, and had a story to tell thereafter, which she did with relish.

The volunteers contributed more than their time, for some of them developed close ties with particular parents and children. A middle-aged volunteer became "Grandma" to two boys who needed and loved the special attention she gave them. A single father with two preadolescent daughters became good friends with a volunteer who had daughters close to the same age.

Volunteers also gave us a broader perspective from their life experience. When I expressed dismay at the waste of food in one home, having observed a large steak about to be thrown away after a few bites, a volunteer remarked, "Of course! She's from a large family. When I got married, it took me two years to learn how to cook for just two of us."

Some volunteers took children into their homes for a day or two in emergency situations. Those in groups provided transportation for group members. Marsha Gordon hosted afternoon tea for families awaiting admission to Cedar House. Some helped overwhelmed parents clean their houses. Local philanthropist Isabel Patterson brought her little dog to entertain the children. One dear senior citizen tended the sweet peas in our yard. Another volunteer established a supply of good used clothing, sorted for emergency use by clients.

Our logo came from the pen of a volunteer, Pat Nekervis. We had mentioned a comment by Supervisor Mary Lee of the Department of Public Social Services, who said of Cedar House, "Things grow faster here." Pat produced a page full of creative drawings, including one of a cedar tree shooting up beside the words, "Things grow faster." We chuckled, then chose the logo of a house and sun. The lettering on the logo matched wood letters that decorated our living room wall.

Perle Chudnow of the Federation of Jewish Women enlisted her organization to scrounge for us, providing needed items. Bernice Cooper, then secretary to Long Beach Mayor Tom Clark, produced a Cedar House cookbook to raise funds for us. Joanne Pearson, a Junior League volunteer, founded a fundraising group, the Friends of Cedar House, and organized the first of the annual fashion shows. She bullied Clara and me into wearing decent dresses for the occasion and paying admission to boot.

Several volunteers became informal lobbyists for child abuse legislation and proposals. Others gave speeches to classes, community groups, and workshops on child abuse and on the Cedar House program. Bob Ward, a man with an interest in city affairs, kept our name before city officials. Later appointed to Los Angeles County's Commission on Alcoholism, he was instrumental in helping us obtain permission to use space in a county building to start our second program, Sarah Center.

A mother once called to ask Marilyn whether wine went in her spaghetti sauce or in the water with the spaghetti. After Clara and Larry experienced the couples' group potlucks, we were delighted when several Junior League members agreed to teach cooking and sewing in a homemaking class. Sometimes the class provided material for therapy as well as for the body. Clara noticed when Paula emerged with an enormous jar of the newly prepared jam, more than any other mother had taken, another cue to her boundless emptiness and need for limits.

Some of the parents reported that they could not recall a moment in their lives that was free of tension. This led to a volunteer's offering a yoga class. It also led to a memorable day when Bo Pearson, husband of volunteer Joanne, joined us to teach relaxation techniques. We staff members lay with the group on the floor, concentrating on our breathing and visualizing. It felt wonderful. As it happened, however, we had also arranged for a foster child to visit with his parents at Cedar House that morning. While we relaxed all over the living room floor, the parents illegally drove away with the child. Our state of relaxation did not last long! Fortunately, the family was found before the day was out.

Several of the volunteers went on to earn master's degrees in social work or education. Emily, a client who later returned as a volunteer, eventually earned a PhD in psychology.

A deep bond developed among the staff and volunteers. Several years after we left Cedar House, former volunteer Nanci Brounley held a luncheon reunion in her back yard. She had planned for us to sit at two large tables, but as we emerged from the house with plates in hand, no one was willing to be separated from the others. We all gathered at one table, squeezed but happy, as we caught up on each others' lives.

It was at this luncheon that we heard what a powerful effect Cedar House had had on the volunteers' lives. One, who had gone on to earn a master's degree in education, remarked that the staff meetings had been "better training than any course I could have taken." Some, having experienced divorces and single parenthood, tearfully told of how they were called upon to use what they had learned at Cedar House. It was a tender day. The years had passed, but the team bonding remained.

Chapter 22

Stages of Treatment

We learned to anticipate some predictable phases as the families progressed through therapy. The length of time for each stage varied. Consecutive stages lasted as short a time as a single session or as long as several months, even a year or more, but there was a consistency in the order of their occurrence.

PARENT STAGES OF TREATMENT

Physical Abuse

The therapy with Cedar House families progressed from a beginning phase, to a middle, and an end.

At intake the parents of physically battered children were usually defensive, depressed, humiliated, overwhelmed with shame, and outraged with the system. Many were in denial, claiming the children had hurt themselves, that the injury was not that bad, or that someone else was responsible for the abuse. Some claimed that the child had to be punished and that the interference of social workers and the courts made it impossible for them to parent properly. Their demeanor tended toward the extremes, either outraged or beaten down. They blamed the system—the police, social workers, the court—for their problems.

In the beginning we stressed providing support and concrete help. We tried to respond to what the parents saw as their needs. When a mother complained of not having a stroller for her baby, we put out the word among our volunteers to find a stroller. While we suggested that they look at what part of the responsibility for their situation was theirs, our initial emphasis was on establishing a base of trust from which to proceed. What we found was that many had never developed the most basic capacity to trust others. Thus the beginning phase of treatment could be a long process lasting a year or even longer.

The concept of personal responsibility was not an easy one for most of the Cedar House parents. Projection and determined blaming of others was deeply entrenched, and not easily dislodged. The bulk of our work in these cases, besides establishing ourselves as trustworthy, consisted of bringing parents to focus on the effects of their own actions on their lives. When they came to some realization that they were at least partly responsible for their current situation, we were in the middle phase of therapy.

Group therapy helped soften the parents' defenses. As trust developed, their dependency needs surfaced in spades. This was when we received frequent telephone calls. There was a tremendous need on the part of these parents to test us: "Are you still there?" One woman sometimes called six times in a day. A mother who lived in the area walked by the house daily, just to reassure herself that we still existed. It was a scary feeling for them to risk trusting us, for they were more accustomed to anticipating loss or betrayal. Their anger level remained high as they waited for the shoe to fall. We did our best to reassure them of our continued commitment while at the same time teaching social boundaries—for instance, when to call on us and when to refrain.

Some therapists questioned whether we were "fostering dependency" by being so accessible, but we saw our efforts as allowing, not fostering, the dependency. Could they learn to be reliable for their children if they had never experienced anyone they could themselves depend on? We hoped that the experience of dependability on our part would model that which they would need to exhibit for their children. We verbalized that with them to drive home the point. We also trusted that they would need us less as they grew stronger. We were delighted when they showed signs of independence and confidence in their own strengths.

During this phase we focused more intensively, though not for the first time, on the dynamics of their families of origin. How had they been nurtured? How would they have liked to have been nurtured? What had they learned to expect of a parent? Of a mate? Of a child? How did this show up in their present relationships? We were simultaneously reparenting, teaching the identification and management of feelings, and helping them to use their minds and verbal skills to understand and deal with present and future stresses. We also continued an intensive sorting out of responsibilities. What led to the harm to the child? Could the parent have prevented the situation? What needed to be done now? The more they showed a willingness to hear another view and to focus on a solution to their own problem, the more they began to see light.

Setbacks were to be expected. Some parents experienced a sudden upsurge of rage when they thought they had gotten past such feelings. This called for either a deeper tilling of ground already covered or the plowing of new ground. Some parents suddenly stopped coming. We made telephone contact, if possible, and followed up with a home visit if we still felt uneasy, for we knew that old patterns of withdrawal and isolation can resurface in times of stress.

During the setbacks clients expressed discouragement and fear of repeating past actions, including abuse. Again they were emotionally inaccessible to their children for a time. We assured them their feelings were temporary and normal for their stage of treatment, that they had not failed us or themselves by feeling this way again, that it would not last forever, and that this could serve as an opportunity for further growth. The setbacks were of shorter duration than the initial stages.

We suggested termination of therapy when we saw them comfortable with themselves and their children, when they had demonstrated an ability to manage their rage without doing harm, when they were less obsessed with crises, and when community supports were in place. Always we left the door open for them to return if they felt the need.

Sexual Abuse

In cases of physical abuse, we worked with the batterers and their mates or significant others where possible. In our work with sexually abused children, we rarely worked intensively with the offenders, who were for the most part no longer living with the children. The thinking of the day precluded having sex offenders in the same program with the children. In our work at Cedar House, later at Sarah Center, and in our private practice, however, we found that fathers accused of molesting preschoolers were often awarded court-ordered visits with the children, sometimes unmonitored. At Cedar House and Sarah Center we referred the offenders elsewhere for their sexual issues, but since some continued in the children's lives, we saw them for parenting issues.

At intake the nonoffending parents, usually weeping, expressed rage and outrage, confusion and guilt. Many were in denial. Most of them were shaken to the core, feeling the world out of control and themselves as well. Many suffered physical reactions and were unable to work. Their sex lives were adversely affected. Role reversals of the parent and child were common, the child trying to protect and care for the parent. Many of the children were in complete control of the household, as the parents were unable to set limits on them. ("How can I discipline them after all they have been through!") Fathers reported murderous impulses toward the offenders. When one said that he would like to kill the perpetrator, I replied that the child needed him at home, not in prison. He asked in a classic Freudian slip, "Wouldn't the court take into account any exterminating circumstances?"

We were at first puzzled by the mothers who suspected their spouses of molesting the child, even when the offender was known to be someone else. We eventually realized that their basic level of trust, the most primitive stage of development, was shaken by the disclosure of the abuse, leading to a deep-seated questioning of their judgment. As they could no longer trust themselves to know where to place their trust, the mistrust generalized to all those around them, including their spouses.

It was only natural that the shaken core elicited an upsurge of unresolved issues from childhood. As the parents experienced the maelstrom of feelings surrounding these issues, they became too overwhelmed and self-absorbed to be emotionally accessible to their children. Therapists sometimes interpreted deep pathology when they encountered the parents in this stage. We learned to expect the extreme but temporary loss of emotional stability among our entire range of nonoffending parents.

While overwhelmed, parents were often reluctant to allow the child to regress, as this too often touched the sore spots of their own childhood issues. Since this was often when the children wanted to regress, the parents were often angry at them. As programs evolved to teach children how to avoid being molested ("Say no, run and tell someone"), mothers of those few who were remolested expressed fury that the children had not done what "they knew" to do, giving the children a double whammy of dealing with another abusive situation amid renewed parental fury. During this phase we continued to work with the children on self-protection but stressed to the parents that it was primarily the adults' responsibility, not the child's, to provide protection. In this stage, with our encouragement, the parents began to set limits on the child's controlling behavior, which they had been unable to do during the initial shock.

Like the parents of physically abused children, as the therapeutic work progressed and denial diminished, the parents of sexually abused children began to face what part they had played in the situation. This elicited increased anxiety and guilt. The parents experienced strong swings in emotions as fears and self-doubts surfaced: Is my child forever damaged? Will my son become a molester? Can my daughter ever have normal sexual relationships with a mate? How could I have let this happen? The focus of the parents' anger shifted elsewhere, from the child to the offender, judgmental relatives and friends, or the system. Families were frequently divided as grandparents defended the offender, refusing to believe he could do such a thing, and leaving the onus on the child. Love/hate polarities were common.

Bit by bit the parents gained confidence in their parenting skills. No longer in denial, they were ready to hear about the abuse. Some were driven to hear every detail, though each new disclosure from the child was likely to send another shock wave through their emotional system.

Eventually, as they learned to trust the children's and their own ability to handle the stress, the parents became more comfortable with themselves and with the children. They began to enjoy their offspring—in some cases for the first time. Others rejoiced, "We're a family again!"

For these parents, too, there were setbacks, producing a cry of "Will it never end?!" If the child or anyone else mentioned another detail related to the past abuse, the parent was likely to reexperience high anxiety, another upsurge of guilt and self-doubts, but for a shorter time. Each setback overcome led to the parents' growing trust in their children's process and their own.

CHILD STAGES OF TREATMENT

Physical Abuse

Physically abused children and sexually abused children demonstrated many of the same characteristics, but there were some notable differences. Anxiety-ridden physical activity was more common among those who were physically mistreated, with some children running aimlessly from place to place in the playroom. Those who frantically stuffed food into their mouths, not stopping for a breath, were the physically abused and neglected children.

Pam remembers the physically abused children as more likely to hit, despite the passivity indicated in student Helen Johnson's research. There was generally a harder edge to some of these children. They demonstrated determination to pull hair or twist a nose, sometimes requiring physical restraint.

Symptoms common to both physically and sexually abused children were the plastic smile, a sadness or flat expression in the eyes, severe nightmares and sleep disorders, bedwetting, difficulty concentrating, and under- or over-eating. As treatment progressed, body language softened.

Sexual Abuse

At intake the children often demonstrated a strong need to be in control, possibly related in part to their parents' stage of being out of control. Small children gave imperious commands. We honored their need to be in charge, within reason, while establishing our guidelines for safety and use of the playroom.

As we honored the children's need for control, at the same time providing boundaries for safety, the children relinquished the battle for total control and regressed, wanting to be treated like infants. As their regression was accepted in the playroom, the children began to disclose what had happened to them. These three stages—bossiness, regression, disclosure—might occur in a single session or they might occur over weeks. Since many of the children had been told not to tell, sometimes threatened with horrible consequences ("Your mother won't love you"), or feared such consequences even if no threat was spoken, the initial disclosures were often accompanied by heightened anxiety, nightmares, new fears, and sadness. The children needed a great deal of reassurance of their safety and of the adults' commitment to protect them during this phase.

Once assured of their safety and that of their family, the children gave information more freely, volunteering details of the abuse. Symptoms of anxiety diminished. Beds stayed dry. Attention turned to more age-appropriate activities and behavior.

As with the adults, the children had occasional setbacks. Earlier symptoms (bedwetting, nightmares) might recur, suggesting an inner struggle. Sometimes the setbacks were followed by further disclosures with more details, eliciting reactions from the parents. Once those memories were aired and worked through, however, the children returned to age-appropriate behavior.

Sometimes the parent(s) and child were more or less in sync as they progressed through the stages of treatment. Other times we became aware that they were out of balance, getting in each other's way. The parent(s) might be driven to hear the details of the molestation while all the child wanted to do was to be held and rocked. If the mother demanded answers, the child was likely to withdraw, feeling less than safe. Conversely, if the mother was in the stage of denial while her child was ready to tell all, the mother's reluctance to hear was a powerful shutdown for the child. We sought to alert parents to what stages to expect and to bring the parent/child stages into harmony.

We found it important to tell the parents and children what to expect of themselves as therapy progressed. With that information they were less likely to see themselves as crazy when overwhelmed by feelings.

TREATMENT STAGES OF STAFF

As the families went through their stages of treatment, we staff members went through our own stages. Our initial phase when we first met abusive families could be best described as the "Oh my God!" response. "That's what it's like? Oh my God!" This was not very helpful to our clients, to be sure, but we had to start somewhere.

Hoping to find a ready answer, we took Donna, who reported her rage out of control, to a consulting psychiatrist. He advised her to blow up a paper bag to regain control. She reported later that she could not find a paper bag when she was holding the coffee table over her head, ready to throw. So much for ready answers!

We tried techniques such as "active listening." This proved helpful for reducing someone's sense of isolation during the therapy session, but did not keep that table from being thrown later at home.

For a time we worked on sublimation and physical outlets. We engaged the clients in exploring what else they could punch when they felt they must punch something. Donna proudly showed us the bruises on her wrist where she had hit the wall instead of the child. We brought in punching bags, and we made stuffed pillows to hit, kick, or throw.

We tried verbal restraints. For some people it was enough to say, "You must not hit that child before I see you next week," or, if we felt uneasy, ". . . until I see you tomorrow." We learned to clarify what we meant by "hitting." When Paula's child arrived with a clearly bruised handprint on his arm, Paula said she had grabbed him by the arm, but he "bruised easy." Marilyn asked her to show how hard she had grabbed the child and ended up with Paula's handprint on her own arm. Paula literally did not know her own strength.

Cedar House tried a variety of approaches. We did a lot of nurturing, offered parenting classes, focused on family dynamics, were introduced to the neurolinguistic approach, and we encouraged exercise and activity to combat depression. We laughed a lot and saw people feeling better.

We became more and more aware, however, that many who were feeling better still had large residues of rage that puzzled and frightened them. In fact, as some of them experienced the sweet times, we witnessed the emergence of anger that they felt for having been deprived of such experiences in the past. "This feels so good. Why couldn't I have had this in my own home?"

Finally, we decided to explore what the parents were dealing with when they spoke of rage. The parents described it as all-consuming, as "it," as though the feeling had a life of its own. We wanted to know just what "it" consisted of. Thus began our exploration of rage.

Chapter 23

Rage:
The Breeding Ground of Violence

We began holding "rage meetings" to find out for ourselves what we were dealing with that resulted in the abuse of children. To our surprise and gratification, the meetings themselves proved to be one of our most effective approaches in helping people deal with their explosive feelings.

A total of thirty-one people—mothers, fathers, and, in one meeting, professionals—took part. In our first meeting, being needlessly cautious, we invited people that we thought were "ready" for it or "would benefit." Thereafter we gave an open invitation to our clients and let them select themselves. Generally those we thought should be there did attend while the more fragile ones stayed away, though a few of the latter surprised us by participating eagerly. Some told us they could not wait to come.

We purposely did not define "rage" for the participants, but asked them to define it for us. When we spoke of "rage," heads nodded and eyes widened in recognition as they responded from their own experience. It was this that we wanted to draw on. The only time we were asked to define the term in advance was in the group of professionals, who were hesitant to share until they had established what *we* meant by the term.

The questions we posed were basic:

1. What does rage mean to you?
2. What does it feel like when you are in a rage?
3. What do you feel before the rage? Can you feel it coming on?
4. What do you feel after the rage has subsided?
5. What triggers your rage? When do you feel it?

6. What helps you stop the rage? How can anyone intervene before or during a full-blown rage?

The clients described overwhelming feelings: "It's like a volcano," "a pressure cooker," or "like a dam breaking and you're suddenly washed into a flood, and you're carried with it until it subsides." They found the feelings (in their words) explosive, violent, overpowering, frightening, crazy, weird, not normal.

Most participants described an urge to hurt someone. A few wanted to disappear or run away, possibly to avoid the more violent urge. Many believed themselves to be crazy, confusing intense anger with insanity. Our language itself makes the association through the dual use of the word "mad." We found it important to help people make the distinction.

The urge to hurt someone led to fantasies, and sometimes actual physical assault or destruction of property meaningful to clients themselves or to those with whom they were angry. For those who viewed children as property—particularly stepparents and boyfriends—the children were natural targets when the urge to lash out at the mate arose. (Rage, after all, is not rational.) Parents' abuse of their own children could reportedly stem from the urge for self-punishment, as well as from anger when the child did not fulfill their needs.

Some described dissociating in the midst of overwhelming rage. One man, Wayne, said he experienced "both fight and flight," doing battle while he viewed the scene "through a narrow field of view from back over my shoulder." Another told of watching himself from both behind and alongside his acting body. The phrase, "I was beside myself," has roots in experience.

So does "a blind rage." We were struck by the degree to which people blocked off their senses. A few told of the inability to see anything but a field of color (literally seeing red—or orange, yellow, black, purple, or white), while some described tunnel vision. Several reported their inability to look at or listen to anyone during a rage. One reported a buzzing in his ears. The visual and auditory sensations apparently served to block out unwelcome reality, much like children's more direct technique of covering their eyes or ears with their hands.

Some spoke of being "out of touch," numb, unable to feel. Wayne, for instance, sustained a broken nose in a fight and was not even aware of it until the next day. Tracy, an aggressive and vulnerable woman with a background of unspeakable abuse, reportedly blacked out in times of rage and had no recall afterward. Another mother commented that in her teens she had felt nothing—she had deliberately cut herself without feeling it—but now that she was regaining her feelings, her rage was "like going through labor."

There was general, though not unanimous, agreement that the participants felt out of control during a rage. Some commented that they did not want to be in control. They appeared to make an internal but unconscious decision to free themselves from an intolerable situation (in their view) by releasing their inner control. One benefit of the rage meetings was bringing the internal permission into the light of consciousness.

Prior to an outburst, the participants reportedly felt tense, hurt, and scared, but some claimed they had no warning, that "it" took over or they "just snapped." Celia, an overweight woman who spoke in a flat monotone, commented that she could not feel it coming before she exploded. Clara noticed her tense body and expressionless voice and asked if she was close to rage at that moment. She replied that she was. When asked how she knew, she said her stomach felt tight. This observation began her process of tuning in to the cues of her body, a helpful step in bringing her feelings under control.

Physical tension was the most consistently reported cue to a rising rage level. People described tension in their stomachs, chests, breasts and hearts, in faces and necks, in jaws and gritted teeth, in their fists, and even in their eyebrows. The tension produced shaking and trembling, heavy breathing, sweating, flushing, tingling, vomiting, stuttering and, in Tracy's case, seizures.

We witnessed Celia in a rage when she argued with another group member after a meeting. She became practically catatonic, standing motionless with clenched fists, frozen, across the room from her adversary, not uttering a word. Both were obviously relieved when Clara intervened. We later asked Celia to rate her rage level in that moment on a scale of 1 to 10. She replied, "Eleven!" That described her feeling level, not her behavior, for she maintained a kind of control by ceasing to act. She had been referred to us for neglect of her children. We suspected that her form of neglect was a similar protective immobility in response to the demands of the children.

When asked how they felt after the rage subsided, three people reported unequivocally that they felt better—relieved, calm, relaxed, mellow, happy—with no mention of guilt or regret. All three had abused their children severely enough to have them removed from their homes, yet outbursts of rage relaxed them! This did not mean they were happy at having hurt their children, but their rage was so intense that the relief from it obliterated any guilt. (There are similar dynamics in those with overpowering addictions.) Two of these mothers described physical abuse and considerable neglect in their own childhoods, while the third described severe verbal abuse without the physical abuse.

Some others reported feeling worse after a rage, while the largest number had mixed feelings, relief from the tension but with regret for the way it was expressed. Most of those who felt worse without the relief had received less or no direct abuse from their parents, although some had witnessed violence or had had traumatic experiences outside the immediate family. Those who felt some degree of relief—wholly or in mixed feelings—appeared to have received more parental abuse in their backgrounds.

We observed that those who experienced the more severe abuse in their early years generally felt the greater relief through the physical discharge of abusing their own children. Those whose own abuse was less severe could also become enraged to the point of abusing, but they felt worse, not better, for doing so. Without the parental model that taught that the total loss of control was to be expected, they felt a greater degree of guilt, for the most part. There are always exceptions, of course. Tracy, who bore scars of repeated physical abuse and was sexually exploited and abandoned in her childhood, reported feeling excruciating guilt when she injured her own child.

Rage reportedly served not only to release tension but also to assert power. Clients could go from feeling totally helpless to feeling able to intimidate. As Paula remarked, "My rage says, 'You'd better!'" Rage was also reported to serve as a barrier against closeness for those who feared intimacy, to stop spousal harassment in the moment, and to signal the need for help and relief from responsibilities.

Defining their rage, people described not only intense anger but also hurt, helplessness, hopelessness, guilt, hate, sadness, and frustration (or "flustration," as some called it). They put the triggers to their outbursts into two categories: (1) the immediate trigger—what "set them off," and (2) the times of vulnerability when they were more likely to be "set off." Those less aware of their vulnerabilities were often puzzled by the triviality of their immediate triggers.

Paula told of flying into a rage when her husband asked why she was putting a particular dress on their daughter. Baffled by her reaction, she dropped in at Cedar House to sort it out. As she talked, she recognized that she was oversensitive to any question of whether she was doing right by their child. She was vulnerable following a recent visit with her mother, who had been critical of her mothering abilities. It took one question in that moment—"Why did you choose that dress?"—for her to blow.

When clients reported a reaction that puzzled them, we walked them through the experience in a play-by-play, tapping their rational mode to rescue them from their confusing feelings. ("When did you first feel this way? What was going on?") Almost invariably the trigger to the reaction became clear.

For the women, criticism of their mothering was a common trigger. The questioning of parenting abilities did not always have to come from another person, however, but could be internalized criticism. "If the child cried, didn't that mean I did something wrong? If the child misbehaved, didn't that show that I am a bad mother?" Then came the twist: "You, child, are making me a bad mother." Rage followed.

A child's refusal to eat was sometimes interpreted as a rejection of what the mother had to offer, particularly for those who prided themselves on their cooking. But children could also arouse rage responses by eating. Paula, with her bottomless needs, could not tolerate her children trying to take a bite of food from her plate. Another child was severely beaten for eating a piece of cake from the freezer. The depth of past deprivation prevented many a parent from developing the ability to share with their children.

Several people spoke of rage that resulted from being laughed at or ignored, an observation that resonated with all the parents. Perceived betrayal—a broken promise, denial of a past agreement, a failure to give support in a time of need—was also described as fodder for rage.

One mother remarked, "The more often you have rage, the less it takes to trigger it." She referred to times with no emotional reserves to help maintain control and when the internal permission to blow up had already been negotiated. Navy wives and a fireman's wife told of their vulnerability when separated from their husbands. Grief and losses that revived past hurts set the stage for outbursts. Some spoke of the rage of being born black and finding themselves viewed as not measuring up to others' standards. Perfectionism with its inevitable path to perceived failure was seen as a breeding ground for rage.

Some spoke of a never-ending state of rage. A father commented that his was "a condition, not an event." Tracy described hers as "like the sun—it rises every day, reaches high noon getting hotter all the time, gradually goes down, and occasionally it may be covered over with clouds, but it is always there." We came to view the constantly simmering state of rage as a result of early neglect and abandonment, the child (now adult) coming to question his or her very right to exist.

Most participants reported that an outburst of rage had to run its course until spent. Only three people reported that they were deterred from giving vent to their rage by fear of the consequences of violence. (All three had hurt their children in reportable offenses.) Most said they lost all concept of consequences once the rage "took over." Some noted that they needed someone to stop them when they were ready to blow up and that their anxiety was massive when there was no one present who could do so. One higher-functioning mother told of a man who grabbed her arms and said, "You cannot do this!" She appreciated his intervention, for it helped her regain control.

Some talked of looking for insights into their own dynamics, but two perceptive women cautioned that in their experience, insights could lead to heightened rage for a time. It had dawned on them that their parents' criticism of them had little to do with their own actions, which clarified that they did not deserve the treatment they received and that fixing the situation was beyond their control. This realization elicited an enormous, though temporary, rage. They cautioned that those in that stage of therapy needed support until the insight was absorbed.

All agreed it did not help them to hear "Calm down!" but some said questions that called for thought, if asked in a noncritical manner, could interrupt the flood of feelings. One example given was "What is it you really want?" The consensus was that what helped most in a state of rage was to be accepted, rage and all, and given permission to voice it.

We found it crucial to assess with the participants their state of mind before they left the rage meetings. Some reported feeling better after airing their darker feelings, but others were more anxious. It was not our intent to arouse anxieties and then send parents home, putting their children at higher risk.

At the end of a meeting, we took the emotional temperature of each participant. When we sensed heightened tension or if some reported feeling tense, we worked with them to spell out what supports were available and what each one planned to do afterward. There was much joking and laughter toward the end, discharging tension. It was always gratifying to see the support the participants gave each other, for no one left the room without several phone numbers to call.

We held one follow-up gathering to assess the effects of the rage meetings. Nine people showed up. The intervening times since their initial attendance at a rage meeting varied from six months to one year and four months. At previous meetings, we had estimated that the participants were fairly evenly divided between those who felt relieved and those who felt more anxious as they brought their rage to light. Five who came for the follow-up had been in the more anxious category.

We asked them to rate their rage level on a scale of 1 (no rage) to 10 (high) at the time of their first meeting and at the time of the follow-up. For the first meeting, all of the participants rated themselves either a 9 or a 10. Two-thirds of them, including most whose anxiety was raised by the discussions of rage, rated themselves far lower at the follow-up, ranging from 1 to 6½. There were three exceptions, however. One woman reported she had felt better after the first meeting, yet she had gone from a 10 to 10½ in her estimate. In her case, she was where she needed to be, for until the first rage meeting, she had been unaware of the depth of her own hurt, though it affected much of her life. When she allowed herself to feel, the rage was initially intense, a not unusual phenomenon.

Two women reported themselves with a 10 at the first meeting and still at a 10 at the follow-up. One, who insisted she was as enraged as ever, nonetheless appeared much mellower than in the past, both to the staff and to the group members who knew her. Her rage had taken a different, less destructive form. She no longer cut herself, but she cried a lot, a behavior she had not allowed herself in the past. We did not trivialize her self-report of pain and high rage, but we were gratified to find her expressing it in a healthier manner.

All of the clients who took part in our rage meetings, without exception, requested more of them. While they had discussed their "anger" in our other groups, it was when we invited them to dissect their rage—that which led to violence—that they found relief. One called it "like lancing a boil." This turned out to be a fortunate benefit of our project, which we had started primarily to help us, the therapists, to understand what we were dealing with.

Chapter 24

Atonement and Forgiving

Most of the clients with whom we worked, adults and children, were loaded with feelings of guilt, deserved and undeserved. Much of our work centered on sorting which was which and dealing with both. As parents joined us in public speaking, eager to promote understanding, willing to tell the world of their own dark deeds, we became aware of their need to atone. We also became aware of their need to be forgiven, a need often stymied by their own inability to forgive. Paradoxically, only as they learned the process of forgiving could they consider themselves forgivable.

Our awareness of the clients' pain from unforgiven hurts, as well as our own need to do some forgiving, led us to examine by what process we had successfully forgiven others in the past. In May, 1992, Clara and I presented the following paper at a National Symposium on Child Victimization in Washington, DC.

To Forgive or Not to Forgive

Victims of child abuse suffer painful effects resulting from the violation of their bodies and souls. Should a victim ever be expected to forgive the abuser? This question can lead to debate and even heated argument among survivors and clinicians.

In the following paper the authors propose to explore the issues of forgiveness, the process of forgiving, and the question of whether it is necessary or advisable to ask it of victims.

During the past eighteen years of treating families in which children have been abused, we have dealt with many deeply damaged human beings, both adults and children. In our experience those who have healed most effectively have been those who have gone through the process of forgiving.

In our minds forgiveness consists of the release and relinquishment of an individual's anger, hurt, hate, and fear toward another person. Forgiving in the face of fear and hurt can be hard work and does not occur in a day. We have become convinced, however, that complete healing does not occur until the work of forgiveness is done.

Contrary to some people's interpretation, forgiving does *not* consist of deciding to stay with an abusive partner, regardless of the abuser's actions. It is, in fact, not possible to forgive completely while the abuse continues and fear remains. Emotional distance is required for the release of anger, hurt, and hate. We do not believe it is possible to achieve the necessary emotional distance while in a state of fear.

Forgiving is, of course, never the first phase of therapy. In the process that leads to forgiving, we see several stages. These we have defined by exploring our own process and by comparing notes with our colleagues and friends.

STAGE 1: SUFFERING THE ABUSE

This is likely to be a time of confusion as well as psychic and sometimes physical pain. Whatever the source, abuse inflicts a wound on the soul.

STAGE 2: RESPONDING WITH A DEFENSE

The victim makes use of whatever defense he or she has developed in the past. A severely abused victim is not likely to lash back for fear of further retaliation. It is probable that he or she will withdraw, try to accommodate, ingratiate, or act out in another setting. We think of adult victims who live behind drawn blinds to avoid human contact. Others smile a lot but develop physical problems. Some find means of getting secret revenge. Marie, the victim of an abusive husband, told of using his favorite towel to clean the toilet, then hanging it back on the rack for his use.

Some victims deny that what is happening to them is abuse. In fact, we have found it unlikely that victims will identify abuse in the absence of outside validation. One man told of his father hitting him on the head with a board "but I wasn't abused." A woman described the severe beatings she received as a child. It never occurred to her that this was abuse until, as a preadolescent, she went to the beach in a bathing suit that exposed her bruises and welts. When she overheard an adult exclaim, "I would never do that to a child!" she realized for the first time that hers was not the usual punishment.

For those who reach adulthood without having recognized the abuse, the first impulse is to deny it. The pain of seeing the parent as having been wrong all along is too great, for the victim experiences the loss of the idealized "good" parent while becoming aware that the suffering of the abuse was not a necessary evil after all.

STAGE 3: AWARENESS OF THE ABUSE

With the loss of the idealized parent comes grief. With the recognition of the abuse comes rage.

The realization that what hurt was indeed abuse may occur at the time or any time thereafter, perhaps years later. Whenever the realization sinks in, anger rises. The victim is forced to recognize that the offender does or did not have the victim's interests at heart. This can be a very painful insight, leading to rage at the abuser (sometimes generalized to society) and to deep-seated feelings of grief.

It is critical to the healing process that the rage, the hurt, and the fear be brought forth and experienced in full. Responsibility must be assumed for those feelings, but in this stage it is not helpful to hear, "You must forgive." Such a statement can in fact be damaging, for the victim, far from being ready to forgive, may take this as evidence that something is wrong with him or her for being so angry.

In this stage the victim needs to hear, "You are right where you need to be" and "You don't have to forgive." It is true. You *do not* have to forgive. In any case, forgiving is not the task of the moment. It is enough simply to feel and to express the pain. The therapist, too, must be able to endure and accept the expression of that pain—not always an easy job.

We do find it helpful to plant seeds of thought. We might say, "The one who hurt you must have been hurt in some way himself. I know that doesn't take away your hurt." Usually the victims are in no mood to respond to an abuser's pain, but seeing the abuser as damaged makes it easier to revise the victims' views of themselves as the defective ones in the equation.

STAGE 4: MAKING USE OF THE RAGE

It is therapeutic for the victim to find some means of empowerment, to diminish the feelings of helplessness and victimization. This is the time to confront the abuser, if possible. Sometimes this stage is characterized by a growing lust for battle, a rising need to confront not only the offender but also others who may be insensitive to one's pain or of an opposing opinion.

The enormous energy of rage can be directed into a socially useful channel with benefit both to the victim and to society at large. Some people become activists, organizing support groups, speaking in public, working to prosecute offenders, etc. Tammy, a survivor of sexual abuse in childhood, a prostitute in adulthood, and a member of an incest survivors group, volunteered to appear on television. She was soon in demand as a speaker. Each time she was interviewed, she appeared to be drained by the experience, yet she continued to volunteer. The experience was clearly therapeutic for her.

STAGE 5: MOVING ON

Eventually doing battle becomes wearing. No longer constricted by fear and feelings of powerlessness, the individual has a genuine option on how to proceed. It is possible to continue maintaining the feelings of hurt and anger. It is also possible to choose to release those feelings and forgive, *not for the benefit of the abuser but for one's own health and peace of mind.*

In our experience forgiveness does not occur without a decision to forgive. This is often brought on by the desire for relief from pain or weariness. Some achieve this state by seeking support from God, "leaving it in His hands." Rarely does forgiving occur in the absence of emotional support from another, validating the individual's worth despite the wound.

In this stage it is important to move toward health, focusing on activities and companions that bring support and satisfaction, rather than outlets for anger. Social activism may continue, but with a shift in intensity.

STAGE 6: FORGIVING

The release of the hurt and anger occurs below the level of consciousness. Rarely can we pinpoint the moment of forgiving, yet we become aware of it after the fact. "I saw the person who did me wrong, and I had no reaction at all." At this point the individual, no longer a victim, is truly free. Jane told of calling her mother and identifying herself, to which her mother replied, "Jane who?" Jane knew she had achieved the emotional distance required for forgiving when she no longer felt rage at this ultimate wipeout. By relinquishing her idealized expectations of her mother, she no longer experienced the pain of betrayal.

With emotional distance one sees the abuser more clearly, uncolored by fear or anger. The abuser is finally recognized as a person, flawed but no longer dangerous to one's own well-being.

STAGE 7: SETBACKS

As in most human endeavors, there are setbacks. When we believe we have forgiven but find ourselves again resenting the hurtful person, there is still work to be done. This is not failure but simply another of those final steps to healing. It usually does not take long to proceed again to forgiveness and healing, presuming there is no further abuse.

If there is another incident of abuse, however, the process begins anew.

If the victim and abuser no longer live together, the victim's growth needs to be independent of the abuser's actions. Thus the victim's progress need not depend on what the abuser says or does. (Nor, for that matter, should the abuser's progress depend on the actions of the victim.) Michelle claimed to be stuck until her mother admitted to being wrong, implying that her own mental health depended on her mother's confession. Ideally, the victim and the abuser may be helpful to each other if the victim confronts the abuser and the abuser acknowledges responsibility and makes amends. The process of forgiving, however, needs to occur regardless of the other's actions.

FORGIVING ONESELF

The process becomes more complex when it is ourselves we have to forgive. All of us have done something in our lives that has caused hurt to another person, something that we regret. How do we forgive ourselves?

Guilt feelings are almost certainly present at some level among young children who have molested other children or who have played a part in harming others. We may tell them that they are not to blame, but they will still need to atone for their guilt.

Most of the stages for self-forgiveness are similar to the stages of healing described previously. We inflict a hurt on another person, usually out of our own pain, self-protection, or ignorance. We then proceed to the defensive reaction: denial ("I didn't do it"), blaming ("You made me do it"), rationalizing ("I did it for your own good"), or self-blaming ("See, I'm no good"). Ideally this is followed quickly by acknowledgment of the guilt feelings and a move to make use of these feelings to motivate our own inner growth. Before the guilt feelings can be fully alleviated, however, we need to find some means of making amends to those we have injured.

Seven-year-old Katie, examined by a doctor and questioned about the identity of her abuser, named a schoolteacher. She later admitted her father was the perpetrator, but in the meantime she was aware that the teacher had lost his job because of her allegation. She felt guilty and needed a means of relieving the burden. With the therapist's help, she wrote a letter to the former teacher, apologizing and adding, "I want to know if you are all right." (We later heard from this teacher, a man who could teach us all about the art of forgiving. He had acquired a teaching job elsewhere.) Katie's behavior improved markedly after she wrote the letter. Once she had made amends to the best of her ability, she released the guilt and moved on, at least for the duration. It remains to be seen if she needs to rework the issue in future stages of development.

We find it helpful with those needing to forgive themselves to reassure them of their place in the human race. Children and adults alike are comforted when they hear, "All of us have done something we wish we had not done, something we feel bad about. You're no different." Then we add, "When we make a mess, we have to clean it up." We explore ways to make amends. Is it enough to apologize? Would it help to write a letter? Can we repair or replace any physical damage? How do we regain trust that has been ruptured? How do we prove we can be responsible after we have behaved irresponsibly? Is confinement called for? Reparations? What will it take to atone? Whatever it takes, it is important to do this work in order to proceed with a sense of being forgivable.

Many adult survivors have internalized their parents' view of them as sharing the blame for childhood abuse or even as the cause of the abuse. "You made me hit you," or "You know you wanted sex." Nor does it take a parent's words to make a child feel responsible for the abuse. The child needs to feel responsible in order to maintain some sense of control in the world. "If I didn't make it happen, then I can't make it *not* happen." The price paid for assuming responsibility is guilt.

Surviving adults may continue to carry those internal tapes and come to despise themselves for feeling helpless and angry. The residual feelings from childhood must be accepted and forgiven before the adult can be relieved of the burden of shame, guilt, and the feeling of being different.

A survivor with some adult coping skills may be able to comfort him- or herself through the inner child. "What was it you (the child) wanted? Can you offer it now? Can you, the adult, stop your child from continuing to punish you, from needing to atone in self-destructive ways? Can you forgive that inner child for feeling so bad?" Through this process of self-nurturing, the survivor may come to accept and forgive his or her hurting self.

If the survivor has not yet developed enough copying ability for self-nurturing, the therapist provides the nurturing model, all the while defining the process. It takes time, but eventually clients are able to help and thereby forgive themselves.

Once the feelings of self-blame and self-hatred are experienced and acknowledged, it becomes possible to progress to the later stages of self-forgiveness: making use of the feelings (perhaps helping others in self-help groups), moving on toward health, and forgiving oneself. This occurs hand-in-hand with forgiving others.

DISCUSSION

We are convinced that intense feelings of wrongdoing and guilt are never fully relieved without the acknowledgment of those feelings. We have seen that an individual who denies responsibility for wrongdoing is doomed to suffer the effects of those misdeeds longer than those who face the experience and learn from it.

In our view, forgiving is the key to healing. It is sometimes extremely difficult but attainable and worth the effort for peace of mind. While we cannot and would not require anyone to forgive an abuser, we consider it important that therapists give credit to the value of forgiving in the struggle for long-term health.

*   *   *

As Clara and I discussed the process of forgiving with colleagues and friends, the one area of disagreement was at what point one would claim to have forgiven. Our stages in the process were similar, but some reported having forgiven at the point they made the decision to forgive, others after they had ceased to feel resentment, and still others only after they had made an effort, successful or otherwise, to reestablish contact with the abuser.

Must forgiving include reestablishing a relationship with the abuser on different terms, bridging the gap? We have seen this happen, particularly among family members, but this, too, we would not ask of victims. Much depends on the past relationship of the abuser and the victim, the depth and the manner of the wound, and whether the abuser is available and willing to accept a different relationship. Should a victim strive for reconciliation at possible risk of further abuse? Some are driven to do so. It is possible that this is a necessary step toward achieving emotional distance. It helps, however, to be strong enough to deal with what may come of it, whether positive or negative.

Atonement, the effort to make amends for one's own past wrongs, is an important element of self-forgiveness. It is not enough for parents to stop beating their children. We cannot trivialize what they have done, nor can we assure them that their actions are "all in the past" when their children show the effects. They need a means to relieve the tension of self-loathing that guilt produces, too often ultimately producing more harm. The atonement can be as simple an act as saying "I'm sorry" or as complex as establishing an organization. Since a child abuse program deals with parents of hurt children, all dealing with their guilt for whatever part they played in the situation, it is critical that opportunities be provided somehow for those parents to atone for what they have done or not done.

The need to atone and to forgive are of course not limited to abusive parents. This is yet another area of commonality with our clients, as we all share the human condition.

Chapter 25

The Empty Cup

We made the assumption that a parent could not give what he or she had not received. If a parent or other nurturing person hugged them when they were children, then it would come naturally to hug their own children; that is, this act would be one that they would associate with parenting. If their parents read to them, it would probably feel natural to read to their children. But if they were not hugged or read to, this was not likely to be part of their parenting repertoire. If they received little or no emotional nurturing, they could have no reservoir, no skills, to draw on for nurturing their children emotionally. We believed it was not possible to drink from an empty cup.

Thus we assumed that when a parent arrived at Cedar House feeling "empty," it was appropriate for the staff to give to that parent.

It was not necessary, of course, for the staff to make a special point to give to every parent, for not all of them were running on empty. For some it was enough to have a staff member's full attention for a few moments. There were days when the parents had more to give than the staff member who greeted them. Some of the tender moments at Cedar House occurred when clients found that they could give to us as well as receive and that everyone, staff included, had hurting times.

There were cues that tipped us off that a parent needed something extra. Some were able to say, "I don't have a thing to give," but more often they did not have the words to express it. Others burst into tears for no apparent reason, stared absently into space, reported no reaction to highly charged events, or filled their emptiness with fights, frequent sickness, drugs and alcohol, overeating, multiple pregnancies, or an internal world of imaginary people.

There were those who could not endure a quiet moment, for that risked a space for despair to rise to awareness. When asked to stop talking for a moment, such people frequently began to cry, or they ignored the request, bulldozing everyone before their barrage of words. They tended to wear out their listeners and perpetuate their own isolation.

Much of the behavior that, in our view, arose from the emotional void was seen by others as manipulative or "playing games." We agreed that the behavior was counterproductive, often self-destructive, and sometimes annoying. At times we confronted individuals on their self-defeating behavior, but when we did so, we learned to recognize along with the client the hurt and rage that could follow the removal of the symptoms—that is, of the client's efforts to dull the sense of being "dead inside." We needed to be comfortable with the client's gradually increasing awareness of emotional emptiness. Without that, a therapist could simply confront the symptoms without supporting the individual through the painful stage of recognizing and experiencing that void. This could be a volatile stage.

For instance, Cora, a simple woman who had been beaten, molested, and abandoned as a child, began to cut herself when her primary therapist went on vacation. The therapist, learning of this, suggested referring her elsewhere. I could relate to the feelings of alarm, for another person's life and health can weigh heavily on those who believe they share responsibility for it. Others on the staff, however, read Cora's nonverbal message to the therapist: "You are important to me." We saw this as progress for her, for it had taken many months for her to form a bond with anyone. The therapist continued treatment with her, helping her to form her messages in words rather than bodily harm. She was not abandoned for expressing, however inappropriately, the pain of the separation.

We did not expect immediate relinquishment of old destructive behaviors—past habits die hard in all of us—but as the emptiness itself became less intolerable, the need for emptiness-fillers generally diminished. Paula, with her world of imaginary friends, needed them less and less as she expressed herself to real people and was accepted by them.

We explored what kinds of giving from one person to another led to an individual feeling more fulfilled. We already knew that acceptance was one of the most powerful gifts we had to offer, but we were looking for specific acts that made a positive difference in the moods of ourselves and others for that day and the next. What helped to sustain us? Once again we looked to our own experience and consulted with our clients.

Many clients reported that the welcome they received as they entered Cedar House was enough to lift their moods, sometimes for the whole day. I knew the power of a welcome from an incident in my own experience. My family dropped in unexpectedly on friends we had not seen for months. When we arrived, their faces lit up with pleasure as they offered hugs. After a pleasant visit, our family went on to another household where we were invited for a large gathering. There a woman greeted me with a cold, sarcastic comment. Normally I would have reacted with annoyance. This day it did not touch me, for I was fortified by the warm reception of the previous visit.

Most of the sustaining experiences that people reported contained a demonstration of caring. One man told of a day when he came to a friend's house to pick up his son. Feeling low, he commented, "I think I'll stay here for three weeks." His friend replied, "Okay." Already he felt better. Both knew that he would not actually stay so long, but there was an implied acceptance: "It is okay to come here when you feel low."

Another father remembered that he could always count on having his mother's attention when he was upset. "It might be just for an instant, but I could count on receiving it." Others also remarked on the power of "being heard." Some mothers reported that it was helpful simply to learn that other mothers were having the same overwhelming feelings, giving them a sense both of being heard by others and of being able to help others through the sharing of strong feelings. It was also possible for them to feel "heard" when they had not spoken. For example, a friend might comment, "You look like you could use a rest." This in itself could be powerful, particularly if followed by an offer to take the children for a time.

Just how effective was respite care in restoring or increasing a parent's ability to give to the child? That depended, of course, on the depth of the emptiness and on how the respite was used. Some parents with a chasm of unmet dependency needs still had almost nothing to give after the child's return. Others might wear themselves out with an unpleasant chore during the respite and still feel empty when the child returned. We encouraged the parents to be good to themselves when they had the chance, for the sake of the whole family. Many of them, feeling themselves unworthy of good things, needed external permission to indulge guilt-free in something pleasant.

One mother, describing a past depression, reported that she found it helpful to talk with other parents in the same boat, but she did not truly climb out of her depression until she went back to school in the evenings. The combination of the respite from parental responsibilities and the involvement in an activity that she valued for herself proved to fill her cup, rather than draining it. She was then better able to mother her children.

Sometimes tangible gifts represented sharing and caring. We looked at whether it was appropriate in therapy to give gifts, for the act could also be seen as manipulative, arousing uncomfortable feelings of being indebted in the receiver. Under what circumstances could and should gifts be given, and how should they be offered?

For people who function at a fairly high level, emotional giving (offering one's time, energies, and attention) creates the most exquisite exchange. Small children, however, when asked what they like about Uncle Fred, are likely to talk about the toy he brought them. Many of the parents in treatment at Cedar House were also concrete in their thinking. A material gift was likely to be noticed more quickly than the therapist's giving of time, energy, and attention.

We gave gifts on birthdays and special occasions, affirming, "We are aware of you, and you matter to us." For those who felt that they did not exist in others' eyes, this could send a powerful message, especially to those who had never received a birthday present.

We gave something concrete to those who were visibly depressed. To accept the gift, the person had to reach out physically to take it. Even in this simple act, we were trying to teach people to reach out in their need, to receive from others.

We gave gifts at termination. This was a tangible symbol of caring and a reminder of the work they had done and the support they had received. It also marked the finalizing of this stage of their growth and the transition to independence.

Sometimes we gave something for the simple pleasure of giving, accompanied by a statement such as, "I just wanted you to have this." We saw this as proper so long as the gift was freely given regardless of the recipient's reaction. Unlike in behavior modification, the object was not a reward for desired behavior, nor was it a call for gratitude. We made some demands of our clients, but not when giving a gift. We saw this as important modeling for parents who were required to give to their children without receiving in kind.

The gifts we offered included such items as bubble bath, food, and items personal to the individual (e.g., favorite color, favorite song, favorite animal, etc.). Occasionally there were practical reasons for a gift. A mother who had trouble getting up in the morning in time for her job became the recipient of a spare alarm clock. Another mother came more often to group therapy after we found her a stroller for her toddler.

The clients' responses to the gifts could themselves be significant. We noted whether they received the gifts with pleasure, discomfort, or indifference. Some felt they must return more than they received. Some absorbed what we gave and asked for more. Some had a hard time accepting anything, feeling they did not deserve it. These clues to their personal relationships often served as material for therapy.

Therapists, too, have varying degrees of comfort in receiving gifts. Being only human, we may find our own buttons pushed: Do I deserve this? What are they after? I am supposed to be the giver around here, but suddenly I am the recipient. This equalizes me. Is that appropriate?

It is important that therapists know their own responses and not always assume pathology to be on the client's part. There are times when it is inappropriate to receive a gift—for instance, when the therapist is about to make a recommendation to the court regarding the client. If such a situation occurred, we would define the boundaries, if we had not done so already. In our experience, this has rarely been a problem. More often it is therapeutic for people to be able to give freely and to receive freely. This is hard to teach without modeling it.

In the years since we left Cedar House, we have come to appreciate more fully the seamless relationship between emotional emptiness and addiction. We had worked with people with addictions, referring them to Alcoholics Anonymous, Narcotics Anonymous, Overeaters Anonymous, and other organizations. In time we developed a keener sense of not only the emotional numbing that we observed but also the spiritual emptiness. We have become particularly attuned to the pain, not only emotional but often physical as well, that accompanies addiction.

To this day we are exploring how the empty cup can be filled.

Chapter 26

Confidentiality

I have written of the early reluctance of social workers to refer families to us, citing confidentiality. More recently, when I suggested that the clients of a child abuse agency have the opportunity to meet a visiting European psychologist and vice versa, I received a similar response of reluctance, again citing the concern for confidentiality. It struck me that the policy of confidentiality, interpreted in this way, serves to maintain the clients' isolation, rather than providing access for them to the community and the outside world.

This led us to evaluate our own guidelines. During our tenure at Cedar House, our concern for confidentiality resulted in minimal records, open to our clients, out of concern that we not be seen as an arm of the court. We did not want what they chose to share with us to be an open book to others. We were against the idea of "staffing" clients (arranging meetings to present or discuss a particular case) without including them to hear what was said. If clients had not given specific permission for us to talk with someone about them, even if we had an unspecified written authorization, we sought verbal permission in advance. An exception might be made to fulfill our responsibility to report child abuse, but there, too, we made every effort to include the parents in the process. We were careful to be open with the clients, not to keep secrets from them, nor even to give such an impression. All these considerations had to do with being trustworthy.

At the same time, we did not want to collude with them in keeping secrets. We made it clear that information was shared with the staff. When they told of family secrets, we honored the confidence, but more often than not, we worked to help them disclose the secret themselves. It took longer, but it helped prevent discord and maintained trust in the long run.

The same held true in our dealings with the children. A therapist once asked how we dealt with children's disclosures, for uncomfortable as it felt, she believed confidentiality required that she keep the children's confidences from the parents. In our view the point of family work was to establish working communication within the family. With preschoolers, we assessed the risk to the child if the parent were to learn of the disclosure. If the risk was low, we shared the information, letting the children know in advance that we were going to do so, and worked with the parents to deal with whatever information was given. Where we sensed a higher risk, we worked with the parents to prepare them for the information at the appropriate time.

With school-age children and adolescents, we honored confidences, but we added that secrets needed to be told sometime in the future and that they would know the right time to tell. I was often amazed at how soon the secret came out—often within a week—after a child had assured me that it could never be told.

In almost all cases, our goal was to have information open and shared within the family, reducing the power of the secret to poison relationships. We were acutely aware, when sensitive disclosures were made, of the need to be available to support both the child and the parent while they absorbed the impact.

These were the confidentiality issues within families. On a broader scale, we obviously did not consider introducing our clients to others in the community and to people from other parts of the world a breach of confidentiality, so long as we did not give out personal information and so long as such activities were voluntary. No one was required to divulge more than they themselves wanted to share.

Until the 1970s, and still to some extent, abusive families could be known to multiple government agencies that rarely consulted each other due to confidentiality. Thus the services rarely had a full picture, services were fragmented, and many clients fell through the cracks. Does our training instill such fears of breaching confidentiality to the point of isolating our clients, or is it we who are by nature more fearful who raise the concern for confidentiality? We have not studied the question enough to offer an answer.

We became more protective of our clients' confidentiality in our dealings with the media. From time to time we were called upon to provide subjects for those producing documentaries or programs for television, to publicize the problems of child abuse. Some Cedar House parents were more than willing to speak before the cameras to heighten public awareness and to offer hope to others suffering the problem. We were not so free to offer access to them, however, after some of their experiences.

Despite our misgivings, Caroline agreed to take part in a program about mothers who had killed their children, with the assurance that she was to be photographed only from the back. The photographer complied, but to Caroline's dismay, when the program aired on television a neighbor recognized her nonetheless.

Sophie, a beautiful and intelligent woman, agreed to be interviewed for a television program. The director, an engaging man, assured her prior to the interview that she would know when it would be aired, and he informed her of the date and time. We all made a point of watching, saw that she had done a good job, and were proud of her for taking this brave step.

Months later, however, after Sophie had gone into business and was on the verge of prospering, the interview was aired again without warning. Some of her customers saw the program and learned that she was the mother of abused children. She was understandably upset.

I put in a call to the director of the show to inform him of Sophie's situation and to ask that the interview not be used again in the future, particularly in light of his previous assurance that she would be informed when she was to be on television. No longer engaging in manner, he informed me icily that she had to "come to terms with her past." My reply was, in effect, "That's easy for you to say now that you got what you wanted, since you're not the one having to deal with it."

Unfortunately for those filmmakers who followed, we were no longer so willing to provide our clients for their purposes. A very engaging young man called us for help with a documentary. We met with him, gave him names and numbers of others in the field, but declined to introduce him to our clients. Linda Otto, who had made the film "Adam," approached us later at Sarah Center but went away empty-handed.

However, not all the families' experiences with the media were negative. Tammy, the articulate and sensitive prostitute who was in demand for television interviews (not through us), felt a sense of accomplishment. Tommy's parents, Wendy and Hal, were thrilled with their moment in the sun. They had no objection to being photographed from the front nor to their young child being photographed. Hal, who had consistently denied breaking his son's arm, startled us by admitting to it on film.

There was one film that did not last, to our regret. In 1977 the Long Beach Child Trauma Council sponsored a training seminar on child sexual abuse. Carrie Reach of Long Beach City College arranged for a filming at Cedar House for training purposes. Jane Gold of the Department of Mental Health's Therapeutic Nursery was to interview several girls whom we knew to have been sexually molested. Executive Director Betty Edmundson of Family Service (then serving as our umbrella agency) expressed concern—an understatement—over the confidentiality issues involved. Those working on the film were careful to get written authorization from each parent for the children to be photographed, and they agreed to destroy the film immediately following the seminar. Only with such an assurance would Betty permit the plan to proceed.

During the filming a ten-year-old girl, working with clay as she talked, carefully formed a penis-shaped sculpture. The camera zoomed in on her creation, recording her concentration on the clay as well as her words as she told of the molestation. With a sudden gesture, she pounded the penis-shape flat with her fist. The effect was dramatic.

Before the seminar Clara sat with the fathers of the girls, who were the admitted offenders, as they watched the film. As she hoped, the film cut through their denial as they saw for themselves how the abuse had affected their children.

The film was shown at the seminar as planned and then destroyed as promised. Many years later we met a woman who had attended that seminar and, unaware of Clara's involvement in its planning, described for us the remarkable film that had opened her eyes to child sexual abuse. She was dismayed to learn that the film had been destroyed.

We had mixed feelings, recognizing both the power of film to reach the hearts of others and at the same time their power to exploit the subjects. We have not resolved our ambivalence to this day.

Chapter 27

Forming a Community Network

From the beginning we were aware that the families needed more services than we could provide. We were also aware that dealing with a problem as complex as child abuse and family violence required community coordination of services.

As part of our effort to develop a network, we held open houses, inviting anyone who might deal with the families and whoever expressed the slightest interest in our project. We went to other settings—to give talks or simply to share ideas. We believed an effective network required a foundation of strong human connections, built through personal relationships.

In one of our first open houses, we invited people to join us and the families as we waited to learn whether we had received a grant enabling us to continue the program. Those who came helped decorate a Christmas tree. Most put on an ornament or two, but Helen hovered by the tree much of the day, glowing with pleasure, for this was the first tree she had ever decorated. Our executive director played with a baby on her lap. Children wandered in and out. Social workers, probation officers, and officials met our families and each other. There was much good cheer when we received the news that we had received the grant.

We all recognized the need for a multidisciplinary group to address child abuse. Early in 1975 Clara and I attended meetings of the Child Trauma Committee, which brought together those organizations that dealt with abused children. The committee ceased to meet for a time, but in December 1975 social worker David Nieman of Long Beach Memorial Hospital revived the concept with California's first child abuse council, the Long Beach Child Trauma Council. Clara was very active in its early years.

Initially we met in a small room of Miller Children's Hospital, but as more people attended, we required a conference room. The name of the group must have appeared too puny for the size of the group, for we eventually called ourselves the Greater Long Beach Area Child Trauma Council. (I have noticed that organizations like to elongate their names.) Finally the group settled on a name that it maintained until this year, the Long Beach Area Child Trauma Council. It has met monthly.

David Nieman and others on the executive committee had an ambitious plan for a citywide coordinated multidisciplinary approach to the problems of child abuse. The plan called for close cooperation among hospitals, county services, private agencies, and educational facilities. Members of the original executive committee of the council—David Nieman of Long Beach Memorial Hospital, Clara Lowry of Cedar House, Arthur Kraft of the Long Beach Unified School District, Jose Martinez of the Department of Public Social Services, and Carrie Reach of Long Beach City College—represented those four categories. They seemed to be ubiquitous in the community, giving talks, providing consultation, and sponsoring parent education symposia and workshops. The initial plan was never implemented in full, but the council has gone a long way toward opening communication among organizations.

In 1977 social worker Connie Michaels and I presented a case before the Child Trauma Council to demonstrate the fragmentation of community services that still existed. As I recounted a family's history of agency contacts, without editorializing, I set up a carved figure to represent each organization and government service that had dealt with the case. I soon had an army of figures lined up on the table. Few of the agencies involved had consulted with each other. The children remained at high risk with their mother, who suffered the agonies and auditory hallucinations of schizophrenia. Both preschoolers had recently been hospitalized with an overdose of the mother's tranquilizers, one child in a coma. They had previously suffered a series of dangerous incidents. Connie's report to the court mentioned among other comments that the floor in the children's home was covered with dirty diapers and flies. A judge started to pass this off as "nothing but a dirty house report" until Connie forcefully argued of the physical danger to the children.

Many of the agencies involved were represented in the audience. By the end of the presentation, emotions ran high, and all agreed that more coordination was needed. While fragmentation was still evident, we had at least developed a forum for the message to be heard and a network of people to call on to address the problems. Over the years it has borne fruit.

The Long Beach Area Child Trauma Council sponsored several seminars in its first decade. The first one, in November 1977, dealt with "Incest and Sex Abuse," long before sexual abuse had become a byword. The panel consisted of local pioneers in the field: Janice Brown of Orange County's Child Sexual Abuse Treatment Team, Ann Chaleff of UCLA's Neuropsychiatric Institute, Michael Durfee of Los Angeles County Health Services, soon-to-be-author Susan Forward of Van Nuys Psychiatric Hospital, Hank Giaretto of the Santa Clara County Child Sexual Abuse Treatment Project, Jane Gold of the Therapeutic Nursery, Roland Summit from Harbor-UCLA County Hospital, and me. Clara served as moderator of the panel, which offered more of a dialogue than separate prepared speeches. The following year the council and the Los Angeles County Department of Community Development cosponsored a two-day conference on sexual abuse, this time including some of the above speakers and adding voices from universities: Alvin Rosefeld of Stanford Medical Center, Alayne Yates of Loma Linda University Medical Center, and Alexander Zaphiris of the University of Houston.

In 1979 a one-day seminar dealt with depression in children, while the 1980 seminar focused on the problems of abused children in the judicial system. The panel in the latter, which included two judges from Dependency Court, reduced several people in the audience to tears. While social workers expressed frustration with judicial decisions that they felt had endangered children, the judges responded that social workers were sending them inadequate reports. The social workers asked for guidelines to improve their reports for the purposes of the court. One of the judges replied, "We can't give a course in law in a few hours!" The social workers felt themselves in a catch-22, given the blame for bad judicial decisions but given no hope of improvement short of acquiring a law degree.

The council's concerns for children in the court system remained high, leading to another all-day, well-attended workshop in 1986 on

"The Interplay Between Legal and Treatment Intervention in Child Abuse." This time legal and treatment professionals demonstrated more respect for each other. The ongoing tension between the two approaches has continued to this day, however. I predict more such workshops in the future.

In 1977 the Long Beach Child Trauma Council and the Long Beach Memorial Foundation cosponsored the making of a film, *A Chain to Be Broken.* David Nieman initiated the project to publicize the problem of child abuse and to encourage the formation of more councils. Bringing the idea to reality was not always a smooth process. The filmmakers of FMS Studios saw the appeal of the subject of child abuse, but when it came to presenting the work of the councils, they were less enthusiastic. The view of a bunch of professionals talking to each other was hardly dramatic enough for their taste. Eventually they were persuaded to find a way to include the message that had been the reason for the film.

The film company showed up one morning at Cedar House to capture our group in action. Clara and I found ourselves wearing microphones in our bras, a new experience. Monstrous lamps and the movie camera hovered nearby, ready to record our every word and gesture. One of the mothers began to cry as she talked, and the group was appropriately supportive. When the session ended, the cameraman was delighted with the "shoot."

In 1984 Clara and I attended the International Congress on Child Abuse and Neglect in Montreal, Canada. As we milled around among the crowd, we were mystified when several people we did not know greeted Clara by name. Someone from New York finally explained that she had seen the film, *A Chain to Be Broken.* She found Clara's comments in the film to be comforting. Her words had traveled farther than we had ever dreamed!

David Nieman's vision for the Child Trauma Council did not stop at the borders of Long Beach. He helped establish the Los Angeles County Coalition of Child Abuse Councils, followed by the California Consortium of Child Abuse Councils at the state level. His and others' efforts to encourage the growth of more child abuse councils bore fruit. At the time of this writing there are sixteen active child abuse councils in Los Angeles County. From time to time we are reminded that the Long Beach Child Trauma Council was the model for those to follow.

After David Nieman left, when the council had difficulty finding people to accept his position, the bylaws were changed to ensure that the vice chair would automatically succeed as chair. Oddly enough, the required two-year commitment proved less problematic, apparently allowing the vice chair a year to get used to the idea of being in charge. Clara served from mid-1979 to 1980, longer than most because her predecessor could not finish her term. I served one year in 1985, the anniversary of our first decade in existence.

During my year in that position, I attended meetings of Los Angeles County's Coalition of Child Abuse Councils and met our counterparts. I discovered that our council had gained a peculiar strength through our annual turnover of leaders. Others complained of difficulty in finding people willing to share the work required to keep the councils going. Our council did not become accustomed to one member to shouldering the whole load. We had a variety of leaders, some stronger than others, but the consistent and structured change strengthened the group as a whole.

In 1996 the Long Beach Area Child Trauma Council and the Greater Long Beach Domestic Violence Prevention Council merged, acknowledging "the inherent links between child abuse, domestic violence, dating violence, juvenile delinquency, and violent crime in general." Together they have since formed the Long Beach Area Child Abuse and Domestic Violence Prevention Council. (I suppose it will be known as the LBACADVPC for short.)

In 1978 we attended a newly formed gathering of people on the cutting edge, the Preschool Sex Abuse Group, a gathering of professionals brought together by Dr. Michael Durfee of Los Angeles County's Health Services. Mike has demonstrated a talent through the years for sensing a rising issue related to children and for bringing people together to pool their expertise. At this time the sexual abuse of children was coming into focus.

The Preschool Sex Abuse Group met monthly and then every two months for a total of eight years. Eventually the group produced a book, *Sexual Abuse of Young Children,* co-authored by Kee MacFarlane, Jill Waterman, Shawn Conerly, Linda Damon, Michael Durfee, and Suzanne Long.

Mike Durfee went on to form the Death Review Committee under Los Angeles County's Interagency Council on Child Abuse and Neglect, focusing on suspicious or unexplained deaths of children. Through his work with Death Review, Mike became aware of the siblings of children killed through abuse and, true to form, he has sought out those working with such families. His most recent group, the Grief and Mourning Group, began as a forum for people who treat children and families traumatized by the violent death of a loved one. Mike has said that the Preschool Sex Abuse Group took three years to get to the topic that was on his mind when he started the group: the need to change the system. He still sees the need.

Our hunger for answers to child abuse has taken us far afield from our little corner of Long Beach into many parts of the city, the county, the state, and the nation. It has brought us into contact with the poor, the middle class, and the wealthy, often in the same day. It has driven us to international conferences in Montreal, Sydney, Rio de Janeiro, Brussels, Hamburg, and Prague. We have learned that some of our problems appear different from the perspective of other cultures. We have also learned that many of our problems are indeed worldwide and universal. Wherever we have been, we have met courageous individuals addressing the problems of child abuse. We are grateful for the forums that have enabled us to come together, reducing our own isolation in the field.

Chapter 28

Funding and Its Effects

Funding is a never-ending concern for any agency, large or small. For small agencies it is a matter of life or death.

Cedar House began with the support of Trailback Lodge, a program for troubled adolescents. Some months later, however, the organization's ambitious undertakings proved beyond its means. The board of directors agreed to continue paying Marilyn's salary for the time being, but they could not afford Clara and me. We found ourselves working without pay for three months, but we never considered closing down.

We well remember the plush carpeting and imposing desk in the Office of Economic Opportunity, where we were told they could not afford us, and besides, weren't we duplicating Family Service? They had no concept of the intensive needs of the population we served, for "child abuse" had not yet caught on in the public mind. Soon after our meeting, their plush Long Beach office folded. Cedar House survived.

In the fall of 1975, the Junior League discovered us. The timing was fortuitous, for they were looking for a new project. They submitted a proposal to their board of directors, calling for a funding grant, a considerable number of volunteer hours, and the administrative umbrella of Family Service. The grant was not large, for neither Clara nor I worked full time. (Clara was paid 60 percent while I received 50 percent of full-time pay.) Both of us worked more than the hours we were paid, but we both needed flexibility in our schedules for family responsibilities.

A Junior League volunteer arranged for us to host a potluck at Cedar House for the City Council members. Eight of the nine council members attended and shared a meal with us, the families, and the volunteers. We were not properly zoned for what we were doing, but this never came into question, thanks to our community support. The next time the city budget was approved, we received some funding from the City of Long Beach.

We continued to hold Christmas open houses. One year a man from the Elks Club, in his fashionable suit and tie, found himself seated next to a woman whose background included molestation, prostitution, and marriage to an abusive man. I was aware of them as I walked by, for she was talking and his eyes were wide. I have no idea what she said to him, but very soon thereafter we received a donation from the Elks Club.

In 1979 we came to the attention of the Interagency Council on Child Abuse and Neglect (ICAN), a recently formed organization with representatives from the county departments that dealt with abused children. Deanne Tilton of the Department of Public Social Services coordinated the efforts to reduce the fragmentation of county services. Until ICAN came into existence, a family might contact the police department, child welfare, probation, adoptions, and the county hospital, none of whom shared information with the others, citing confidentiality. Deanne skillfully guided the process as department heads relinquished some of their territorial claims.

ICAN sought a model agency for the treatment of abusive families in Los Angeles County. Deanne learned of us through Roland Summit, and in 1979 Cedar House was chosen to be the model for the county's Neighborhood Family Centers.

Meanwhile two dynamic women had formed ICAN Associates, a private organization to raise funds for the Neighborhood Family Centers, creating an experiment in public/private partnership. Elaine Trebek, the former wife of game show host Alex Trebek, and Bourne Morris, an advertising executive, were cofounders of the group. We received visits from Elaine and from Christina Crawford, author of *Mommy Dearest,* who became one of the leaders in ICAN Associates.

Bourne Morris arranged for a visit to Cedar House by a representative of Mattel Toys Foundation. We invited a few mothers to join our meeting. As our guest observed us, Emily and Jennifer of two different groups described what Cedar House meant to them. Comparing notes, they became so absorbed in each others' comments that they appeared to lose all awareness of our presence for the moment. They played a large part in persuading our visitor to recommend our program for funding.

The ICAN Associates added color as well as finances to our lives, providing us with the experience of several elegant fundraising events. When Clara and I attended a planning meeting for one of ICAN Associates' fundraisers, we found ourselves on the fringe of the world of Hollywood. We were amazed at how much time went into a debate over the color of the balloons. Yet those present, concerned as they were with balloon colors, were also concerned for children, some having suffered abuse themselves. The event they planned, featuring Dudley Moore and a blind child playing on two pianos, was a huge success.

From time to time we received word from Family Service that they could no longer afford the administrative services for us. While the problems of abused children tugged at people's heartstrings, the hunt for funds was ongoing and the paperwork never ending. Executive Director Betty Edmundson looked tired. The board of directors were clear that their first priority was, reasonably, the Family Service program, not Cedar House. We were pressured to hire people with degrees that would lend more prestige and credibility to the program, enhancing our marketability. This pressure led Clara and me to apply for our licenses in the spring of 1978, and it also led to our loss of Dr. Larry Hanna, when his name and title went into the Family Service brochure against his stated wishes. He announced his departure at the next staff meeting, to our stunned regret.

Several times we prepared our families for the closure of Cedar House due to the lack of funds. Each time something came through. We found, however, that the repeated threats of closure had a subtle effect on our investment in the program. When we worked without pay, we were faced with the possibility of failure, but our emotional investment stayed intact. The second time, the question arising once more, we began to prepare ourselves to say good-bye. Rescued again, we were still able to reinvest our energies in full. The third time, however, we began a process of grieving and relinquishing. Those who have grieved only to learn that a loved one will unexpectedly survive know both the relief that follows and the need to readjust. Our staff went through this more than once. It took a cumulative toll.

What saved us from the last near-closure was a grant from Los Angeles County in 1980. When the grant came through, the Family Service Board of Directors decided the time was right for Cedar

House to become an independent entity. We were in the odd position of interviewing candidates for the executive director of the agency that employed us. The first one to join us, Bill McCue, did not stay long but moved on to an offer with better pay. He was succeeded by Freda Hinsche.

Oddly enough, the larger grant that allowed us to hire more staff proved to be our undoing, disturbing the delicate balance we had maintained. Clara had always been clear that she could not work full time and maintain her family responsibilities. This was accepted so long as we had little money with which to pay a program director. Once the money became available, however, county officials and Freda Hinsche agreed that the program must have a full-time program director. One day Clara was stunned when Lynn Seiser, hired as a therapist just a few months earlier, came down the stairs and announced to another person in the room, "I'm the new program director!" Clara had agreed to train someone for the job, but had no forewarning of the timing of the change nor of the choice for her replacement.

With a new executive director, a new program director, a newly formed board of directors, and several newly hired staff, all with their own ideas and agendas for how to proceed, power struggles began. We had grown accustomed to those who told us what more we should be doing when we were sparsely paid and using all our energies on the program we already had. We were not used to this kind of struggle, however. Suddenly we became expendable, thanks to the new funds. Clara chose to resign. Marilyn and I stayed longer, hoping to salvage some of what we had built together, but it was clear that our era at Cedar House was coming to a close.

The program has been through hard times since then. We are gratified to know that it has continued to serve families, thanks to the determination of caring people, and that its community support has not diminished. In 1996, Cedar House merged with Sarah Center, a move that makes sense, for as we noted long ago, physical and sexual abuse are partners. For those Cedar House staff members who left to lick their wounds in more turbulent times, we hope all have found peace.

What advice can we offer in retrospect? Build slowly, with an administrator who understands the team concept, and do not lose sight of the purpose of the program. And pray a lot.

Chapter 29

Program Feedback and Client Update

In late 1979 an effort was made to evaluate the Cedar House program for replication in other settings. The plans did not materialize as envisioned, due to changes occurring in Cedar House at the time, but we did receive feedback from clients and community representatives who were interviewed. Their comments were recorded in a "Descriptive Analysis" in January 1980.

CLIENT INTERVIEWS

Five clients from each of three categories—new, ongoing, and terminated—were randomly selected by outside observers for interviews. Only four interviews actually took place with the ongoing and terminated clients, giving us a total of thirteen client interviews. New clients had been with Cedar House for two to three months, ongoing clients for six months to two years. The analysis failed to note how long the terminated clients had been with Cedar House nor how long ago.

The clients were asked a series of questions:

1. Have you learned [did you learn] anything about yourself since coming [when you were coming] to Cedar House? A total of twelve people said yes; one (a terminated client) said no without elaborating.
2. Since coming [when you were coming] to Cedar House, have you noticed [did you notice] any changes in your mate? (Not every client interviewed had a mate.) six yes; zero no.
3. Since coming [when you were coming] to Cedar House, have you noticed [did you notice] any change in your child(ren)? ten yes; three no.

4. Since coming [when you were coming] to Cedar House, have you noticed [did you notice] any changes in your ability to cope with your daily living conditions? twelve yes; one said no, but added, "Now we [husband and wife] communicate in place of screaming at each other. We aren't screaming at the child."
5. Have you ever reached out [did you ever reach out] to Cedar House for help? Did you always receive help? twelve yes; one no. (The exception was a new client.)
6. Are there [were there] any ways Cedar House can help you [could have helped you] in addition to what is [was] already being done? eight yes; five no.
7. If you had to do it over again, would you still come to Cedar House? twelve yes; one no.

New parents indicated that they received effective help in gaining an improved sense of self-worth ("I am not as imperfect as I was led to believe"); a reduced sense of isolation ("I'm not the only one this happens to"); help in handling their children ("I have learned to deal with problems that children have"); dealing with anger ("To think first before I do anything to my son or break something"); and expressing and handling feelings ("It is okay to want to murder him. I can accept the anger.").

Ongoing clients also spoke of the improvement in their self-image ("I used to think I was a bad person and I found out I'm okay"), with related comments about becoming more sociable, more open, more assertive, and learning to help others. They noted progress in handling their anger and becoming freer to express feelings. They told of being better able "to deal with my problems" or "handle stress." They no longer mentioned the child as a problem. One told of a new ability to call for help. Another said, "I can forgive myself and grow a little."

Terminated clients focused more on the help they had received in sorting out relationships: "Helped me understand my relationship with my wife [and] with my father." One learned "why I was mad at my mom. I was having problems with barriers I couldn't get over . . . that disappeared after working with these things." Some spoke of learning how to communicate and what to do with feelings: "I learned I could love." They referred to improvement in their self-image: "I started going to school, stopped being a recluse. I was so ashamed for so long. I just wanted to stay at home and hide. This was a major change."

Two new clients saw their mates as the primary problem, but those in the other categories made no such statements. When asked if there had been any change in their mates, in fact, an ongoing client replied, "I take more responsibility for what is happening in our relationship instead of blowing up right away."

All of those who commented on their mates reported changes for the better. A new client said, "She is allowing me to fit into the family now. She is allowing me to be a father." Others said their mates showed less anger and more effort to listen. One stated that "he treats the children differently. He doesn't whip her any more." A terminated client reported, "He grew a little slower than me, but he grew. He made tremendous progress."

Two new clients noted their children's improved behavior at bedtime and better sleeping habits. In four of the five families, the children were reportedly more relaxed, talking more, and handling their anger more constructively. One said, "He doesn't get into his parents' bed now, which has been very beneficial to the marital relationship."

All of the ongoing parents saw less fear in their children. Two indicated the children were more affectionate and sociable, while one reported a child more willing to follow the rules. One was said to have learned to ask for help.

The terminated clients were evenly divided on the question of whether the children had changed. One was critical of Cedar House. "Parents and children should be together to discuss the problem, not separate." Another saw no change but did not elaborate. The other two respondents reported a definite change. One said, "Not at first—two months later I was shocked. [He] talked instead of screaming. My child said, 'You're not listening to me,' and I learned about his feelings." The other reported, "The boy went from being overly concerned with being an animal, [to] slowly realizing he was a human being. From total withdrawal to gradual openness. Cedar House got him into Therapeutic Nursery, which is the best thing next to Cedar House."

All except one who reached out to the program reported receiving help. The exception was the terminated client who felt that Cedar House had not helped her with her child. Ongoing clients found Cedar House "always willing to help. Always have an answer or help to find an answer." A terminated client commented, "It took me a year, but then I could call them. I felt better even before [the] conversation was over. I had trouble asking for help."

Suggested improvements included more home visits and a larger parenting class. A new client said, "There are many people who . . . are very positive and supportive, but it's hard to get the courage to make the initial contact. If someone had gone to my house, it would have been easier. I had to walk though the door, afraid of their reactions." Ongoing clients were concerned that the program continue to be there for them in the future (this being a few months after we thought we might have to close). Some terminated clients expressed a desire for help with current needs: respite care for the children, dealing with social workers, finding a job.

All but one, a terminated client, stated they would return to Cedar House if they had it to do over again. "I wish I knew about Cedar House earlier." "Great program and I would recommend it highly to any other parent who needs that kind of help." "They saved my life—I am alive!"

RECIDIVISM

There was one case of reabuse among the forty-three new families admitted to Cedar House during the six-month period of observation. Two children from that home were taken into placement. In the same period seven children returned to their parents' homes.

COMMUNITY INTERVIEWS

Eight community/agency groups responded to phone interviews: the Department of Public Social Services, the Long Beach Probation Department, the Long Beach Police Department's Child Abuse Unit, Long Beach Memorial Hospital, the Long Beach Court's Juvenile Division, the Long Beach Unified School District, the Long Beach

Area Child Trauma Council, and the California Consortium of Child Abuse Councils.

The unanimous expressed opinion was that Cedar House was doing a good job ("excellent," "outstanding," "no bad reports"). The respondents knew the agency through personal contact, professional interaction, and, in one case, "I have seen many cases, being a judge in the child abuse department for four years." One said, "I have referred several people to Cedar House with good results."

The only reported problems were that "often Cedar House is full" and "I need more information so that we can know how many families Cedar House can take. I would love to refer all clients with this problem to Cedar House." Six reported no problems.

Community people cited a variety of strengths of the program: the counseling services, the caring staff, the parenting class, the immediacy of help, the willingness to shed preconceived ideas and learn from the parents, the therapy for the children, the fact that parents and children were seen both together and apart, and the nonjudgmental and accepting approach to the families.

The main suggestion for change was the need for expansion. Two noted the need for more space and the fact that Cedar House could not "take every referral." One advocated more community awareness of what Cedar House was, possibly because the local newspaper continued to refer to it as a residential shelter. Two found no fault, one remarking "It's one of the most important resources that Long Beach has had in years."

The referring agencies did their own screening of those they sent to us. The respondents looked at the location of the family, how "needful" the family was, the potential and motivation for change, and the likelihood of their sustaining treatment. "[Given a] court order for counseling—first on the list is Cedar House. We involve Cedar House in cases of sexual abuse as they are better able to handle them." A referral might not be made "if the family said no," if the child needed protective custody, or if the client was psychotic.

RECENT CLIENT FOLLOW-UP

Clara and I heard from seven former Cedar House clients, six women and one man, as we worked on this book. Six were asked to fill out a questionnaire to review whether Cedar House had made any difference in their lives and if so, how. Their length of time in the program ranged from two to three months to three years, all but one having participated for more than a year. They were represented in mothers', men's, and couples' groups, in family counseling with their mates, their children or both, in individual therapy, and in the parenting class. All had attended parties and social events. All but one had done public speaking, appeared in television documentaries or, in one case, testified before state officials in Sacramento. One of the seven had attended a rage meeting.

Most of the children had attended group therapy and had participated in family sessions, and all had experienced individual sessions. All took part in the parties, and one had gone on a whale watch organized at Cedar House. One child, then age eight, joined his mother in testifying before state officials. His mother told us that the experience had given him confidence and that he remembered it with good feeling.

Responding to the question of what had been most helpful to them, the parents' replies focused on the staff's attitude, the setting, skill-building, and peer support. Comments included the following:

- "Having someone that understood."
- "People's attitude when you didn't feel your best."
- "The house atmosphere."
- "Learned to protect myself and children."
- "Preparing us for court and letting us talk about our fears."
- "Being with other people who had similar problems—being able to identify."
- "Everything. It really made a big change. . . . Because if it hadn't been for Cedar House, [my husband] would be dead by now. I would have killed him. . . . So Cedar House made my marriage stronger, [my husband] is alive, and I'm not in jail for killing my husband." In a personal interview, she stressed that she was not speaking lightly, remembering how close she came to stabbing him.

When asked to comment on what was least helpful, most wrote "nothing" or left it blank, but the man emphasized his point: "I haven't any negative words whatsoever for Cedar House." A mother wrote, "Knowing it would never go away"—this written in a time of anguish as she awaited the penalty phase in her adult son's trial for murder. When asked what changes she would make in the Cedar House program, she wrote poignantly, "More parent-with-child talks."

Two others had suggestions, both indicating the need for more skilled handling of the transition when Clara and I left Cedar House. One suggested follow-up therapy after going to court. This would normally have occurred, but this family apparently fell through the cracks after our departure. Another mother wrote, "Once trust is established, don't change therapists without client o.k." In an interview she told of the succeeding group leader telling the members, "You just have to accept that Clara and Bobbi aren't here and I am your therapist." She walked out and never returned, angry with both the new therapist and with us. Yet she ended her questionnaire with "Thank you for my life!"

We asked for the respondents' most memorable moments. Some were specific:

- "The day we had race discussions."
- "In group when Marilyn stood and made [my husband] sit on the floor and she stood on the coffee table and yelled at him. That was when the change in [him] came about. He finally understood what it felt like."

Others responded with more general statements:

- "Realization that people . . . *cared* for you in your state of chaos and were willing to stick by you and help in spite of the ugliness of the matter."
- "Learning to be myself and to protect myself."

Some of the changes in their lives that people attributed to Cedar House included the following:

- "I learned to speak up and how to get out before it's too late in bad situations. I'm not quiet any more."
- "I learned to feel rage and identify it before control is lost. I don't hit, I give time-out, and we talk and express feelings. More communication and freedom to *be*."

- "I like me! I can look people in the eye. No one can hurt me again."
- "Much more open and helpful. Learned how to have a more open and loving marriage and family. Still married. Not in jail for killing my husband."
- "I began to accept responsibility for actions I chose to take. I became more aware of other people's feelings—and respecting them, no matter how young. I ceased using violence as a means of expression. Peace now as I've never known it could be. . . ."

WHERE ARE THEY NOW?

Caroline's feedback to us is described in Chapter 15. The family is together and reportedly doing well.

Lily, the mother of another child who died from abuse, has borne three more children, two of them now teenagers in school. All live with her and her present husband. After her work at Cedar House, she chose another partner who hit her, but this time she left immediately when the violence began. A former welfare recipient, she is now employed and has been happily married for seven years to a man who has not been violent.

After many years without contact, Lois made a point of finding Clara before moving out of town. She wanted to let us know the family was still together and doing well. Her husband had initially been harsh with their son, but he had changed. She told us proudly that the boy grew into a loving father of his own child.

Clara ran into Rick, the singer, by chance and learned that he is single and still pursues his music. He composes and has become known among other renowned musicians.

I met Tracy through the tragic circumstance of her son's trial for murder. He had been removed from her after she left Cedar House, which was more than a year after our departure. He spent the remainder of his childhood in foster homes and is now serving a life sentence with no possibility of parole. Tracy is living on the streets.

When Joan, a divorced parent, came to Cedar House, she had three young children whom she subsequently raised while working full time. All three children have attended college. Joan is now a grandmother.

Margaret's four children were removed during our time with her and sent to their father after an incident of reabuse. Abused yet again, the children went on to live in a series of households. Margaret is now raising a second family of two children while trying to deal with troubling questions from the grown children about their upbringing.

Margaret's feedback was especially articulate. Describing her background as totally lacking in nurture and appropriate guidelines (even including her mothers shooting at her), she said of herself and the other group members, "We were babies. You were surrogate mothers. You were doctors, delivering babies. Delivering grown-ups! Y'all taught us how to love." She added, "The only reason I didn't die when they took my children away was you wouldn't let me! I would have killed myself."

Margaret was eager to share her views of the helping professions. She mused, "What you guys did was from what was *in* you, from heart. Those who are following guidelines are going by what somebody else says. It's not the same. . . . They tell you not to get involved, but how can you help us if you don't get involved? I see some who try to be friendly, but they are afraid of us—outside and afraid." Asked if she thought Cedar House could be replicated, she replied, "Yes, replicated but not formatted. It would take special people."

In 1996, Margaret brought us a poem:

Then and Now

It was scary, hard and raw;
We did it by the book,
Faced it, confessed it
We did what it took.
Open your soul,
Remake your mind,
But . . . that was then.

Now. . . .

More open hearts,
More open hands;

Now someone understands.
Remake my mind,
Show me how;
Each child is mine, some way, somehow
To protect and guide
With love is my Now and
That, too, was different
Then than now.

RECENT COMMUNITY FEEDBACK

In December 1996 I received a call out of the blue from Bernice Cooper, the former mayor's secretary and one of our strongest supporters. She called, she said, to tell us, "Those years at Cedar House were the happiest of my life. That sounds strange when you think about hurt children, but I think it was the healing in the atmosphere that made that time so special. I just wanted to tell you."

We were already aware that the healing of Cedar House was not limited to the families we treated. It served as well for volunteers and staff—ourselves included.

Chapter 30

So You Want to Start a Program?

It is almost always true that the work a group does is second-
ary in importance to what happens to individuals who are
doing the work.

—Anthony Campolo,
Ideas for Social Action

This chapter is for those who have thoughts of starting a new
child abuse program. We offer the following suggestions, some of
which were included in the 1980 descriptive write-up of Cedar
House:

Formulate your ideas and your philosophy. What services do you
believe can be helpful in alleviating child abuse? How will you
provide those services? Where will you look for financial support?

Your treatment philosophy will underlie every decision you
make in the program. The philosophy needs to be positive rather
than negative, the work centering around healthy change in families
rather than around child abuse per se. This emphasis on health
rather than pathology needs to pervade the entire program.

It is useful to put your thoughts in writing to clear your mind and
to alert you to any gaps in your thinking.

Tell your plans to anyone who will listen. If there is a need for
such services in the community and if there is heart in your presentation, you will find support, sometimes in surprising places. Others—
not just those in high positions but those with any kind of experience that bears on the problem to be addressed—often have valuable
suggestions on how to proceed. Even the naysayers bring up ques-

tions that need consideration. You do not have to take their word for it that your ideas will not work, but it can be useful to be forced to think the project through in more depth.

By talking with people in the community, you will learn what is already being done or not done, as well as who else you need to approach. Those interested in such a project may be found in community councils, self-help groups, the medical field, charitable organizations, or among educators, government leaders, business leaders, and law enforcement personnel. We were not acquainted with the movers and shakers in our community when we began Cedar House, but we met many of them in the course of our work as one supporter led to another.

Enlist a group of committed people. The core group can be any number of people from any segment of the community. The unifying element must be the commitment to treatment and the dedication to develop a program run with and for the families.

A grassroots program is not likely to thrive if run by professionals who listen only to each other. At the same time, we have seen some self-help groups flounder when operating with little or no professional input. An effective child abuse program requires an orchestration of professional and grassroots people working in concert, none dominating the others, not necessarily singing the same song but producing a harmony. Since the tone of the work is set by the leader, it helps if this person is one whose strength flows from commitment to the families' needs, not from the need for power. (Sometimes you can tell the difference by the size of the administrative desk.)

It is also necessary that the administrator function from both the right and the left sides of the brain; that is, at both the intellectual and emotional/creative levels. Those who operate almost exclusively from the left brain (intellectually) will be out of tune with an intuitive staff. Those who operate almost exclusively from the right brain will find themselves out of tune with the practical needs of the agency.

Locate an informal setting. The facility is important because the building itself becomes part of the treatment process. We are convinced that a house setting, where possible, is best for a child abuse program's purpose because it represents a domestic environment for working with problems of a domestic nature. It should be decorated nicely but not in an extravagant style that would be intimidating to families. Hand-me-downs and run-down second-hand furniture should be avoided unless they can be properly integrated into the whole. In any case, do your best to avoid an uninviting sterile or shabby setting. If you are stuck with the latter, you can enlist a volunteer organization and some of the clients to help renovate it.

Where possible, a person or couple residing in the home adds a nurturing element to the program. The ideal would be an older couple who has raised children and enjoys being around people.

Join with or establish a nonprofit corporation. The latter is not as complicated as some believe. You will need to write articles of incorporation and bylaws and identify the officers of the board of directors before registering the nonprofit corporation with the state. When we started our second agency, we borrowed articles of incorporation and bylaws from another agency and modified them for our purpose. This did not require the services of a lawyer.

Clara and I have had the experience of starting two agencies, one under another nonprofit agency and one that we incorporated ourselves.* We have discovered advantages and disadvantages in both approaches.

A program within a larger agency may have a broader range of available services. There is less likelihood that the program will operate in isolation as the staff comes in contact with others in the agency. In addition, administration costs are reduced, and it is possible that the staff's time needed for fundraising will be reduced. (Do not count on it, however. At Cedar House we still had to spend considerable time raising funds.)

The potential downside of being a branch of a larger agency includes the possibility of conflicted goals if the parent agency and the program have somewhat differing agendas. The survival of the program itself is in others' hands, even as the administrators and

---

*When we incorporated, we found ourselves in a catch-22 position. We had been offered a setting in a county building to start the second agency, but the county required our nonprofit corporation number before approving us. To acquire the nonprofit number, we had to list our address. We were in limbo for weeks but weathered it by using the county address as though it were already approved.

board of directors may be more distant from it. Under another agency there is likely to be more required meetings to attend. At Cedar House, as our program became better known, Clara found that some board members of Family Service became annoyed that our program attracted more attention than the parent agency.

The advantages of being incorporated separately included having more control over the program, and deciding who could be served and what meetings to attend. There were not as many people to answer to and thus fewer conflicting demands, although some of the funding sources had their own requirements. We had no identity problem when on our own. Previously, the parent agencies had expressed annoyance when we identified ourselves with Cedar House rather than Trailback Lodge or Family Service.

The drawbacks of the separate incorporation included having more administrative duties. We also saw more potential for withdrawing into an isolated program, especially as the demands for services from our limited energies mushroomed. It was more tempting in a separate agency to develop an inflated view of ourselves.

Staffing. Ideally the staff should be multidisciplinary, including at least one licensed clinical social worker; a marriage, family, and child counselor; at least one psychologist who can do psychological testing in addition to therapy; a part-time educator; a child specialist; at least one paraprofessional with life experience; and a doctor or nurse on call. You will probably find consultants—a psychiatrist, dentist, nutritionist, financial expert, lawyer, or whoever—as needs arise.

Most important is the ability of the staff members to work as a team. They need to be warm and caring but also be able to set limits. While inclusive thinking opens up many possibilities amongst the staff and volunteers, it also requires judgment. If someone brings a destructive dynamic into the staff—speaking against others behind their backs, shirking the work, demeaning the clients, creating a pocket of hostility—this must be dealt with immediately and, if not alleviated, the staff member must go. Failure to deal with the situation will inevitably affect the services to the clientele, who have sensitive antennae for tension of any kind. Each agency must figure out its own procedures for dealing with such an eventuality.

To hire staff, professional or otherwise, we recommend that an applicant fill out a questionnaire or at least address questions such as the following in an interview:

1. Tell us about some work you have done. Can you describe one of your cases? (We listen for whether the clients come alive in our minds, whether there is a tone of caring, or whether we hear too much jargon, pat techniques, or demeaning of clients.)
2. How did you handle anger with your clients then? How do you handle it now? What do you do when you encounter raw rage in others? (Those without some familiarity with and confidence in their capacity to deal with their own and others' anger or rage will have a hard time in the child abuse field.)
3. What has been your experience working in a team? Doing crisis work? Dealing with suicidal clients? What would you do with a mother screaming into the telephone that she is going to hurt her child?
4. What kinds of abuse have you yourself suffered? How have you dealt with that so far? (This seeks to give an idea whether the applicant can relate to the parents' past histories and how likely is it that countertransference issues will surface in the course of therapy. We would not expect to probe personal issues in depth, but it is important to have some information besides a work resumé for one who is to enter this emotionally charged field.)
5. In your past experience, how have you balanced your intuitive self with the intellectual knowledge gained from your training? (This question may well give the interviewees pause and would provide an opportunity to see how they think through something that calls for more than a pat answer. It may also give a clue to whether they have a working respect for paraprofessionals who have not shared their training.)

Establish a treatment program. Because the treatment revolves around the needs of the families, the treatment program requires a degree of flexibility. Typically the program elements will include group and individual counseling, modified play therapy for the children, a parenting class, and outreach services. Other program components, added as client needs arise, may be twenty-four-hour crisis intervention, helpers in the home to assist with homemaking, respite care of the children, and classes for stress reduction, nutrition, budgeting, anger management, and the like.

Enlist help from volunteers. Willing hands can come from many sources: volunteer organizations such as the Junior League, volunteer referral agencies, student organizations, senior citizen centers (many a retired person loves to hold babies), businesses, and people you know. You will need a training program for the volunteers, covering communication skills, the program philosophy, and what to expect of abused children and their families.

Those working directly with families should commit to a period of at least six months to provide the continuity necessary for this work, and they should attend staff meetings. We also recommend monthly meetings, preferably with food, for volunteers to share their stories and feelings about the work. Some will have strong reactions that may need defusing. These are opportunities for ongoing training, offering more understanding of a family's behavior. Awarding certificates of appreciation is a nice touch, but the more important function of the gathering would be to hear their stories. We tended to do this informally on a day-by-day basis, but we see the value of assuring a structure for the purpose.

Be goal-oriented. Stay true to your purpose, whatever you have chosen it to be. Do not get side-tracked by those who want to address tangential problems, as urgent as they may be, nor by those who prefer a less anxiety-producing approach. ("I don't have time to do home visits!") You will meet those who are quick to criticize but are not found in the trenches.

If you stay focused on the purpose of the program, your clarity should help steady you through those days when self-doubts arise. Working with chaotic families will sometimes challenge your skills to the limit. You will inevitably come upon situations beyond your experience and training. Remember your purpose, count on the team in the days of confusion, and think of those times as preparing a pathway to new ideas.

Invite people and serve food. Luncheons and open houses in which we served food put people at ease, no matter what their station in life. One of our favorite parts of the work was hosting a broad range of people, all ages, all colors, all types, and all social classes from welfare to wealthy, and seeing them respond to each other with interest and enjoyment. Sharing food broke the ice, giving us all something in common as we gathered. When the families were included, the events helped break through stereotypes on both sides. As a bonus, they also helped open people's pocketbooks in support of the program.

Establish community contacts. It is important to establish solid ties among community agencies that deal directly with the families in the program: social workers, police investigators, probation workers, and local hospital personnel. An ongoing relationship with these and other community members provides an important referral source for new clients and also provides avenues for working through client problems as they arise.

At the risk of repeating ourselves, look for a child abuse council in your area. If one does not exist in your community, plan on forming one.

Attend conferences and accept invitations to speak. You may find yourself challenged by the audience at times, but that, too, provides opportunities to deepen your thinking. In the process, you will learn what others are doing in the field and what has worked for them.

Funding. We made a decision from the start to charge no fees. We knew we would serve low-income families, some of whom would not be able to pay a dime. We wanted no barrier to services to those families in which children were at risk. While some have argued that services are less valued if not paid for, this was not our finding. We recognize that with a different kind of clientele or when addressing a problem where lives are not at stake, there is no reason not to charge fees.

To start a new program, it is helpful to enlist the support of local government leaders, charitable organizations, businesses, foundations, and all interested individuals—not necessarily in that order. When approaching them, be prepared with an articulate (but not cut and dried) statement of the need for the services, your philosophy, your purpose and goals, and your plans for achieving the goals, preferably set down in writing.

Our own experience demonstrates a range of resources for maintaining a program. The Long Beach City Council (government) provided funds for us with a minimum of paperwork required. The Junior League (volunteer organization) did likewise and gave us volunteers as well. When we needed a house renovated for our second program, volunteers from one of Long Beach's largest employers, McDonnell Douglas (business), donated materials and provided the labor on weekends to do the job. As people played a part in the existence of the program, they had an interest in its continuation.

It is important, of course, to engage the talents of one who is skilled at writing grant proposals, for both government and private funding requires that the need for and the use of the funds be described in detail. It is through grant proposals that more substantial funding may be achieved. One problem with receiving a large grant, however, is that other potential sources then may assume the agency is no longer in need, ignoring the fact that the grant is time-limited.

Dealing with several funding sources simultaneously can itself cause problems. The paperwork can multiply to a discouraging degree, especially with government funding and its need to track the taxpayers' money. We also found that some who provided grants had their own ideas of how we should operate. When imperious messages came from more than one source at a time, it became interesting, to say the least. At such times we reviewed our purpose to determine which proposed changes would work just as well or better and which would not be true to our reason for being.

It is a temptation for agencies to follow the funding; that is, to change the direction of a program based on what grants are available. We resisted this tendency. Perhaps that is one reason why we are now in private practice.

Integrity is the key. To maintain the trust of the families and of the community, it is important to be absolutely honest about what your program can and cannot offer.

As you venture into developing a new program or adding to one that already exists, you will undoubtedly make some mistakes, and you will receive criticism for them. If, however, your efforts relieve a burden or provide healing for those you serve, you will have done well.

Chapter 31

Adapting the Program

We were fortunate to serve in an informal setting with a small, compatible staff, numerous volunteers, and some thirty-five to forty families in treatment at any given time. The question arises: How adaptable is such a program to other settings?

The basic philosophy. The most important element of the Cedar House experience, as we see it in retrospect, was the mind-set. We were there to learn, which meant relinquishing preconceived ideas and listening to our clients to determine what could help, what actually worked for them, and what did not. We sought to include the parents in our planning and activities in the community, to let them know they had a contribution to make. We learned that people, even those that some called "low-life," can grow and long to grow, though their fears often get in their way. This stance should be adaptable to other settings, if given support by the administration.

Showing the clients they matter. A program that does not seek to allay client fears is itself standing in the way of growth. Some signals (efficiency without warmth, annoyance, ignoring) that indicate, "You are not important here. You must behave in a certain way, even though it may be foreign to you, or we cannot treat you," arouse the very fear that blocks growth. Growth is encouraged by cues that say, "We are glad you have come. We will be with you as you find your way to a path that is more comfortable for you and your family. You can do it." That may be conveyed in as simple an act as a smile, but it is also helpful to say it in words.

As finely attuned as this population is to phoniness, however, the message must be sincere. It is permissible to show a human side with a less sanguine comment such as "I'm having a bad day. Don't worry. It's not you." This alerts them to the staff member's momentary state of mind while relieving them of guilt or self-doubt they might feel due to their less cheerful reception. It never hurts to be honest with these families, so long as the honesty is built on a foundation of goodwill.

Signals can be subtle. As I have mentioned, we moved toward arriving clients to indicate both a welcome and that we were prepared to deal with whatever problem they brought with them. In settings with a seated receptionist behind a desk, even the simple act of leaning toward the clients can give newcomers a greater sense of being valued. People who lean down toward young children send a message of interest in what they have to say.

Keeping close to the appointment time also indicates that the individual matters. I once volunteered to run a videotape for a session in another setting. The family and I waited for an hour and a half past the appointment time while the therapist had a casual lunch. The implied message was that her time was important while ours was not. I was not inclined to return to give further of myself. Why would a client feel differently? For those who are a captive clientele, required to participate, such treatment simply underscores how little they are valued.

Intakes. With crisis-prone families, we believe that intakes should be the beginning of the therapeutic and reparative process. Intakes must focus not only on the presenting problem but on what the program has to offer toward solutions. We do not recommend the more impersonal system of an intake worker who takes down information and does not see the family again, leaving them in limbo until they meet their therapist and have to explain again what brought them to the agency. It is difficult at best to engage some families in a treatment program. If we create another hurdle in their way, we are likely to lose them.

Intakes conducted by teams of at least two, preferably more, compatible staff members can not only benefit the families but can also serve to enhance staff cohesion and diminish burnout. (Problems shared are easier to bear.) It should be possible to arrange for clients to be interviewed by several people, whether the staff is small enough to include the whole team or whether it needs to be divided into several interviewing teams.

Team treatment. How to arrange for ongoing contact with a team is another question. If the client is in a group with cotherapists, that is a start. Clients in more than one mode of treatment (group, individual, parenting class, etc.) will probably be familiar with more than a single staff member. Team home visits acquaint the families with several people on the staff. Parties, picnics, work parties, and special occasions (with guest speakers and the like) that include both staff and clients provide opportunities for getting acquainted, particularly if there is a shared task. It is important for these families, who have grown up for the most part in dysfunctional situations, to see the staff operating as a team, not as diverse individuals who can be played against each other.

To accompany clients to other settings, a familiar team member other than the primary therapist may be appropriate. As the volunteers filled in for us on occasion, we noticed that the parents sometimes felt freer to share things about themselves that they might have withheld from the therapists, since we were perceived to play a part in decisions about their children.

Advocacy. While accompanying clients to other agencies is one way volunteers can serve, we believe it should also be a part of every therapist's repertoire. Time-consuming it may be, but it is eye-opening. We cannot really know what an experience is for others unless we are willing to walk beside them. Ideally all staff members of child abuse agencies should accompany clients at times, both for the support of the families and for the education of those of us presuming to do treatment. In some cases, an advocate's presence may smooth the path. If nothing else, the staff will see how others operate and possibly cement community relationships. They may even pick up some pointers for their own work.

Rage meetings. In child abuse programs and those dealing with any kind of family violence, we strongly recommend meetings that focus specifically on rage, for there is never a dearth of people seeking relief from their explosive feelings. The time required for such a meeting is minuscule compared to its impact. While some therapists have expressed fear of evoking or enhancing people's rage by focusing on it, our experience has shown that clients welcome the light shining upon it. We have had no incidents of an outburst of violence during our meetings. We also recommend, however, that the participants be self-chosen, for they sense when they are ready to explore their darker feelings.

The setting. The homey atmosphere we enjoyed may be difficult but not impossible to achieve in more institutional settings, particularly by paying attention to the cues of the five senses. Comfortable chairs and sofas are a must, preferably including one that allows sinking in with a kind of tactile envelopment. Hard-back chairs are essential, however, for those with back trouble. Murals and paintings are wonderful, but I always look for a decor relating to the purpose of the agency. Teddy bears, kept in reach, appeal both visually and tactilely. A display of children's drawings, parent-child posters, photos, and mottos can serve for charm and as a reminder of why the program exists. When Cedar House moved into temporary quarters after the house burned, the staff and families covered the glass front doors with the childrens' handprints. Though located in a business district, the place could not be mistaken for an industrial center.

The aroma and taste of coffee, hot cocoa, or spiced cider appeal to most adults. Coffee and tea should be available to clients where they can help themselves, to give them some sense of being a comfortable part of the scene. Juice or hot cocoa for the children serves the same purpose. Even if the budget does not allow the extra cost, we have found coffee and cocoa mix to be among the easier items to obtain from donors.

As always, the clients themselves are the best ones to say what helps them feel at home. Ask them.

Ingredients for a model child abuse program. The essential ingredients for an effective outpatient child abuse program are a caring and competent staff with the ability and the opportunity to function as a team; an inviting setting with as few visible barriers as possible and that signals a welcome of the clients; therapeutic components, typically including groups, individual therapy, parenting classes, and other classes according to need; some kind of arrangement for twenty-four-hour crisis intervention; a community network of services able to share information; the conviction that the families can be helped; and the commitment to seek out answers.

Given a faith in the clients' desire and ability to grow and a willingness to listen to them, any agency is likely to find its own unique means of providing effective help. We suggest making use of your own life experience, reviewing who has helped you most in your own unhappy times and how they did it. Incorporate that into your program, along with your training, and listen closely to your clients to determine if it is helping them. You may need to factor out the clients' tendency to say what will please you by comparing it with their actions, but trust yourselves. If your goals are clear, your commitment unshakeable, your integrity intact, your training solid, and your own life experience accessible, your work will bear fruit.

Chapter 32

What We Would Do Differently Today

When I posed the question recently to Clara, "What should we tell others that we learned from our experience at Cedar House?" she replied instantly, "Get a lawyer!" On second thought, she said more seriously, "Be single-minded to your purpose." We went on to review what we would do differently today.

The treatment team. The team is the key to an effective program, but it is not always easy to tell who is truly in sync with the vision of the founders. As we look back, we see mistakes that we made in the process of hiring—not that we hired bad or incompetent people, but our process was not the best.

One mistake we made was to do too much talking in our interviews of prospective professional staff. Too often we told too soon what it was we needed, and the interviewees, understandably anxious to get the job, gave back to us what we wanted to hear. Those who later had a hard time with the Cedar House approach had some heart for the work, but the Cedar House model demanded a different style of relating to clients than did much of their training, which called for keeping more distance between themselves and clients. While some staff members thrived on our approach, the transition was not an easy one for others. Perhaps expecting too much of those with professional training, we were not always wise in our treatment of them, relying too much on an assumption that they would operate intuitively. This was especially hard for recent graduates, who had come from a milieu in which they had to operate at an intellectual level.

Today we would do more concentrated training to prepare the newly hired for what to expect and what would be expected of them. We would work with those who were uncomfortable with our approach to find a setting better suited to their talents, for we recognize that there are many ways to be helpful to people. Given the importance of the team dynamic, we could not afford to continue long with those who were unhappy with us.

By contrast, we did a better job with the volunteers, who had not been trained to keep quite so pronounced a professional distance. They filled out questionnaires in advance and received training geared to the Cedar House approach.

Another mistake we made was to hire a group of new staff members in a short space of time, creating a different dynamic before allowing them to integrate into the program. This resulted from our receiving a funding grant coinciding with a pressing need for expanded services. The newcomers tended to band together, some of them to find fault with us. They may have had a point. We were tired from struggling to keep the program alive while serving families with a staff that was stretched too thin, and we had little energy to focus on their needs. A concentrated session of training might well have prevented problems. In any case, we would bring people on board at a slower pace another time, requiring a period of formalized training, and we would include a probationary period in the employment agreement.

While the volunteers were enthusiastic about our staff meetings, which were quite informal, we learned that one of the newly hired professionals, a psychologist, dreaded the meetings. We generally brought up our concerns about particular families and considered what steps to take. She was used to prepared case presentations, discussed professionally by professionals. In the give-and-take of brainstorming with little apparent distinction between professionals and volunteers, our titles gave us no leg up. Though a lovely person, this was not her cup of tea, but we had not picked that up in our interview with her. Perhaps an earlier questionnaire or training period would have helped.

Treatment. There was very little in the treatment itself that we would change, but a few thoughts come to mind. If we were not dealing with sexual offenders, we would provide more opportunities for therapists to see the men with their children. While we often had the children join us in the adult room to talk or to deal with specific issues, today we would include more frequent occasions for the parents to be in the playroom with their children. We did that, but not enough.

With the sexual offenders, we might prepare them and the children for a meeting in which both would have the opportunity to say what they needed to say in the presence of one or two third parties. In recent years I have had children write or dictate letters in their own words to the offending parents or stepparents, asking the questions that were on their minds and leaving space for written replies. This practice tends to be a reality check for a perpetrator, who is faced with the fact that the child is a real person who has been left with reactions to his acts. (One man reported being "terrified" when he saw his stepdaughter's questions, which to me appeared fairly mild. His hands shook as he wrote his replies.)

For the most part, as we look at what we would do differently, we think of expanding the program rather than changing it. As more twelve-step programs have come into being, we have made referrals to such self-help groups as Narcotics Anonymous, Adult Children of Alcoholics, Adults Molested as Children, and others. We have always encouraged attendance at Alcoholics Anonymous and, when it was flourishing locally, Parents Anonymous.

We would make efforts to find an art therapist, a dance therapist, and a massage therapist who is attuned to victims, particularly those of sexual abuse. While some professional organizations question or even prohibit touch as a part of therapy (sometimes with good reason!), those who have been physically or sexually abused often have a problem feeling comfortable with the bodies they live in. Both a dance therapist and a sensitive massage therapist can be helpful in locating areas of body tension and in helping the healing process.

We would provide classes for the families on subjects such as post-traumatic stress disorder, attention deficit hyperactivity disorder, and other therapeutic issues as they arise. Most abusive families have massive trauma in their backgrounds. A class on post-traumatic stress disorder might help them tune in to their symptoms and reactions, possibly providing relief for those who consider themselves crazy. It would also focus on what past abuse could produce in their children's behavior, giving the parents a better idea of what to expect and a more sensitive view of the child. A class on attention deficit hyperactivity disorder might also alert some parents to a possible cause of their children's infuriating behavior. Some will go on to question whether they suffer from the condition themselves.

We would do more with psychological testing. We resisted the idea at the time, not wanting fearful parents to feel like test subjects under a microscope. Since then, however, we have engaged adults in helping to evaluate for themselves whether a diagnosis or description fits them. During a session we may bring out the *Diagnostic and Statistical Manual of Mental Disorders* (Fourth Edition) of the American Psychiatric Association, read a description of a particular diagnosis, and ask, "Does that sound anything like you?" The individual can then acknowledge, consider, or reject the description, looking at the parts that fit and the parts that do not. We may then explore what the diagnostic word means to them. We will not use the word with any finality by assuming that once we have the diagnosis, we know who this person is. In our minds, a diagnosis should not simply be applied *to* people but considered *with* them.

Of course, we would try to stay true to our conviction that the families were the ones to teach us. Whenever possible, we would add to the program what the families indicated was a need.

Networking. Although we did a good job of networking with the community, for the most part, we had some gaps. We would have liked to have better links with the local medical community. We became acquainted with several school nurses and a pediatrician or two through the Long Beach Area Child Trauma Council, and we involved several pediatricians in individual situations at Cedar House. Occasionally, however, we wished for readier access for a quick opinion and some training on skin discoloration or other symptoms.

We would also have liked more interaction with teachers. We met school nurses and the school psychologist Arthur Kraft at the Long Beach Area Child Trauma Council, but the teachers were already in their classes when the meetings took place. Some sought us out to give talks in classes, and we occasionally sat in on meetings in the schools, but we did not have a natural channel to get information from the very people who spent so many hours with the children. Perhaps we should have formed a support group for teachers dealing with abused children or those suffering from burnout.

Chain of command. One thing we would never do again is to hire an executive director to be in authority over us. This should not be the function of the treatment staff. In our case, as the founders, we were reluctant to relinquish that choice, but we would not do it again.

We had operated with circular thinking; that is, decisions were made by the whole team sitting around the table, each participant considered equally important to the discussion. The Executive Director of Family Service was busy with a full slate elsewhere and interfered very little with our process. An executive director on the premises introduced hierarchical thinking into our program.

As the laws are set up in the state of California, the system requires agencies to think in hierarchies: a board of directors, an executive director, program director, staff. Look at any organizational chart, and the lines lead down, not across. The salaries reflect the considered importance of the position. When we chose the executive director (with board approval, of course), we did not fully realize to what degree we were relinquishing the program. So far we have not found a means to maintain circular thinking in a hierarchical society for more than a few years, regardless of whether the executive director is chosen by us or by the board of directors.

In 1990 I visited a child abuse program, the Kinderschutz Zentrum (Child Protection Center) in Berlin, Germany. There the laws allowed the treatment staff to serve as the board of directors. The staff members took turns chairing the board, hardly their favorite part of their work. Nonetheless, as I observed their high morale and remarkable diversity of activities with a relatively small staff, the visit reconfirmed my belief that people can give a great deal in an atmosphere of team decision making and empowerment.

While we made some mistakes, the experience of Cedar House enriched our lives beyond the words. We hope that others can learn both from our successes and our failings, that others will experience some of the joy that we felt in the work, and that hurting families will find the help they need.

Chapter 33

In Retrospect

Neither Clara nor I had our licenses when we began Cedar House. Neither did others we knew in this beginning field in the mid-1970s, yet some were doing exciting work.

Our university training in human development and family dynamics has been invaluable in our work. I do not believe, however, that a college degree is required to provide effective help to another human being. In recent years I have heard therapists remark that child abuse "is such a specialized field." Specialized? We were dealing with families in pain. We had no classes and very little literature to go by when we began. We learned by listening to the clients and by comparing our experiences to those of others who were also tackling the problem. While I have found wonderful ideas in the ever-increasing volume of writings on child abuse, I am concerned that the talented Marilyns and Pams of the world, those paraprofessionals without degrees but with special ability to make empathetic connections with the walking wounded, may be left behind.

Clara and I were always sensitive to whether other professionals included or excluded Marilyn as we discussed our work. While some recognized her remarkable talent for dealing with emotionally troubled people, others who claimed expertise in child abuse showed little interest in her views. The former were more welcome among us.

*　*　*

We have heard it argued that the child abuse population does not do well at parties because, given their lack of social skills, conflicts arise. We can only say that those who responded to our questionnaire remembered the parties with special pleasure. As the families were welcomed with warmth, the participants joined in the festive atmosphere. When a rare conflict did arise (I can think of only one occasion, involving an angry father), the families saw us in action as we dealt with the situation, taking him aside to defuse his anger. It was important, of course, that all had a sense that there was someone in charge. To our knowledge, no one left feeling uncomfortable.

*   *   *

Early on, we met those who wanted to broaden the agency's goals to include "domestic violence" in our efforts. We were indeed dealing with violence against women and in a few cases against men, but we were still struggling to convince the public that children were abused and needed protection. We decided to keep that as our focus, not because we were unconcerned for the battered adults but because we had seen time and again how easy it was for adult needs to take priority over those of children.

In recent years the fields of child abuse and domestic violence have started to merge. Now that child abuse is accepted as a genuine societal problem, our concern that the children will be overlooked has diminished somewhat. We will continue to watch, however, to see whether adult suffering overshadows that of the children.

*   *   *

To minimize burnout, we staff members validated each other rather than laying on more pressure. As often as possible, we used Friday afternoons for play and laughter, even as we reviewed the families' situations prior to the weekends. We offered each other time off for healing when the inevitable sadness of the work proved momentarily overwhelming. Out of concern for each other, however, we did not abuse the privilege of a day off when it was likely to be at the others' expense.

A few staff members hired in later times were delighted with the idea of mental health days. The overuse of this practice necessitated establishing a policy and procedure for time off, which reduced our flexibility. We saw then how bureaucracies begin. We loved the work we were doing, but we were not good bureaucrats.

*   *   *

I have written of the memories that we cherish, of a few adventures we would have preferred to do without, of the laughter and tears of our work. I have neglected to report, however, the fatigue and the depths of sadness that we experienced as well. This was extremely demanding work, sometimes haunting us at home when we felt a child could be in imminent danger of harm. We were fortunate not to lose a child who entered Cedar House on our watch. There were incidents of reabuse but none as severe as the abuse that first brought the child to our attention.

For those who are administering similar programs or serving on boards of directors, please bear in mind that those on the front line need emotional backup as well as financial support. Disagreements can be fruitful if aired and resolved, deadly if left to fester. Where there is a diversion of energy into discord, the families will ultimately suffer, for the staff will have less to give. And this will inevitably be the case if staff members are not valued by those who make the decisions concerning them.

*   *   *

We have seen an apparently inevitable tension between front-line providers who deal daily with the needs of the people who come for services and administrators who deal daily with the needs of the agencies. Neither can continue without the other, yet their agendas can differ, leading to discord if basic respect for each other's role is lacking.

In 1988 Clara and I attended the International Congress on Child Abuse and Neglect in Rio de Janeiro. There we met Sara O'Meara and Yvonne Fetterson, the founders of Children's Village (now called Childhelp). They commented that they were the only founders they knew of who had managed to keep control of their program, but they had had to go to court twice to do so.

In the world of hierarchical agencies, the executive director is the key to whether treatment staff is respected by the members of the board of directors and vice versa. We have pondered what can be done systemically to alleviate situations in which the executive director and the treatment staff are in conflict.

It is the natural tendency of board members to support the executive director, at least in public. The newly formed Cedar House board did so when Clara was suddenly replaced as program director with no warning. Cedar House suffered a period of turmoil following our departure. We realize that executive directors need backup as well as other staff members, but if the executive director tends to encourage division rather than reconciliation, a board's support can increase the rift and harm the program.

We see a need for a communication channel that includes the staff, the executive director, and the board of directors—the team concept again, all working in concert. Perhaps one board member, someone with sensitivity to people, could be assigned to meet with the administrator and the staff on an occasional but ongoing basis. If all is well, such meetings should be a pleasure. If there are problems, the board of directors should have some awareness that all is not well. Such meetings should be for the purpose of hearing all concerned and seeking resolution, not to scold, punish or lay down the law on one side or the other. In hierarchical thinking, too often the tendency is to put someone in their place, leaving a residue of resentment. In circular thinking, the idea is to share and, if necessary, to reconcile differences.

Founders, who would not be there had they not possessed a commitment to provide a needed service, are particularly vulnerable when agency needs start to supersede client needs. They fare best when working with an administrator whose response to problems is "How do we find the funds to provide what our clients need?" rather than "We don't have the money, so it can't be done."

* * *

We have been aware that those who follow founders do not have an easy row to hoe, particularly where the program has made a name for itself prior to their arrival. They naturally want to make their own mark, but they bump into the loyalties of friends of the founders. Their inclination then is to blame the founders for interfering. I decided when I left Cedar House that I would not speak against anyone there. The new staff had many a struggle, but the program survived more than twenty years, eventually to join with Sarah Center under the umbrella name of For the Child. Both programs continue to serve.

* * *

As different organizations came to our rescue, I was fascinated by their portrayals of the history of Cedar House. I have read that the Junior League founded the program. I have read that ICAN found "a struggling young program," our entire experience to that date reduced to one phrase. In more recent write-ups of Cedar House's background, Marilyn played no part, for Cedar House was founded by "two social workers." The tendency to erase much of what preceded one's own experience was a mystery to me. Then I discovered myself doing the same thing.

In 1975 we attended several meetings of the recently formed Child Trauma Committee at Memorial Medical Center of Long Beach. Betty Richards, a classmate from USC, served as the chairperson at the time. For ten years I believed that Betty had started the Committee. Then in 1985, when I served as the Chair of the Long Beach Area Child Trauma Council, I learned that Dr. Harry Orme, a beloved pediatrician, was the actual founder of the Child Trauma Committee.

I realized then how easy it is to overlook what happened before our own arrival on the scene. This is one reason, among others, that I have written this book: to ensure the ongoing existence, if only in people's memories, of what went before.

*   *   *

An oft-quoted African proverb says, "It takes a village to raise a child." By focusing on families, we created a kind of specialized village. Given a conviction that it can be done, there is no reason Cedar House could not be replicated many times over for the benefit of communities, families and, of course, the children.

Index

Order Your Own Copy of
This Important Book for Your Personal Library!

CEDAR HOUSE
A Model Child Abuse Treatment Program

_____ in hardbound at $29.95 (ISBN: 0-7890-0146-2)

_____ in softbound at $19.95 (ISBN: 0-7890-0432-1)

COST OF BOOKS_____

OUTSIDE USA/CANADA/
MEXICO: ADD 20%_____

POSTAGE & HANDLING_____
(US: $3.00 for first book & $1.25
for each additional book)
Outside US: $4.75 for first book
& $1.75 for each additional book)

SUBTOTAL_____

IN CANADA: ADD 7% GST_____

STATE TAX_____
(NY, OH & MN residents, please
add appropriate local sales tax)

FINAL TOTAL_____
(If paying in Canadian funds,
convert using the current
exchange rate. UNESCO
coupons welcome.)

☐ **BILL ME LATER:** ($5 service charge will be added)
(Bill-me option is good on US/Canada/Mexico orders only;
not good to jobbers, wholesalers, or subscription agencies.)

☐ Check here if billing address is different from
shipping address and attach purchase order and
billing address information.

Signature_____

☐ **PAYMENT ENCLOSED: $**_____

☐ **PLEASE CHARGE TO MY CREDIT CARD.**

☐ Visa   ☐ MasterCard   ☐ AmEx   ☐ Discover
☐ Diner's Club

Account # _____

Exp. Date _____

Signature _____

Prices in US dollars and subject to change without notice.

NAME _____

INSTITUTION _____

ADDRESS _____

CITY _____

STATE/ZIP _____

COUNTRY _____ COUNTY (NY residents only) _____

TEL _____ FAX _____

E-MAIL_____

May we use your e-mail address for confirmations and other types of information? ☐ Yes   ☐ No

Order From Your Local Bookstore or Directly From
The Haworth Press, Inc.
10 Alice Street, Binghamton, New York 13904-1580 • USA
TELEPHONE: 1-800-HAWORTH (1-800-429-6784) / Outside US/Canada: (607) 722-5857
FAX: 1-800-895-0582 / Outside US/Canada: (607) 772-6362
E-mail: getinfo@haworth.com
PLEASE PHOTOCOPY THIS FORM FOR YOUR PERSONAL USE.

BOF96